Authenticity and Imagination in the Face of Oppression

Authenticity and Imagination in the Face of Oppression

—Monica Joy Cross—

RESOURCE *Publications* · Eugene, Oregon

AUTHENTICITY AND IMAGINATION IN THE FACE OF OPPRESSION

Resource Publications
An Imprint of Wipf and Stock Publishers
199 W. 8th Ave., Suite 3
Eugene, OR 97401

www.wipfandstock.com

PAPERBACK ISBN: 978-1-4982-3944-8
HARDCOVER ISBN: 978-1-4982-3946-2
EBOOK ISBN: 978-1-4982-3945-5

Manufactured in the U.S.A.   09/21/16

Life lives and moves in the midst of her witnesses, compelling each witness to a knowingness of the intimate within.

Contents

Preface

As long as white supremacy is the root discourse, and by this, I mean the discourse of negotiation, mediation and exchange in the United States, American cultural and societal constructs in regard to gender, sexuality and racial identity will continue as usual. Power, privilege and presence as defined by white supremacy will continue to rule the day. If true lasting change and transformation is to occur, this discourse, i.e. the theological, ontological, political and economic ground established to support white supremacy must change. What is called for is a new and different ground of legitimacy.

I write these words as one who is black, a woman, and transgender. I also acknowledge and embrace the masculine in me. I live my life as a black transgender woman who embraces the term queer as a matter of sustainability. Queer in the context of this thesis acknowledges a particular depth of who I am as a part of a progressive liberative discourse regarding gender and sexual identity. Born and raised as a black male I found that my inner being was incongruent with living as a black man. Yet, innately knowing the norms and the requirements to mirror them, I sought to be "obedient" to those established norms. In the long run those norms, at least for me, were not sustainable. Coming out then in my life was about two things (1) sustainability and (2) authenticity. For all of the challenges I have encountered, I cannot sustain that which is not authentic; it's just not in me.

That said, living authentically and sustainably, however challenging, compels me to acknowledge both the feminine and the masculine as real and present, with narratives which critique the narcissistic tendencies of American culture and society—specifically in regard to gender, sexuality and race. Clearly, I and those similar are a threat to the identity regime established by and for the production of white supremacy. I am mindful of the cruelty embodied in the institutions as well as the people indoctrinated by those institutions regarding the transgender person and the black man. So, I find myself to be in a pickle then, either way—as a black transgender woman or black man—I just don't mirror the approved identity framework approved and codified, even legalized, by the political, social and cultural descendants of Willie Lynch and their agents. I find it fascinating that my experience of gender and sexual identity is similar to race as they seemingly emerge from the same regulatory spaces of limitation, fear and hatred.

The two are intimately related, framing critical difference, the ground of authentic queer life, for some, as a betrayal of normative sensibilities. That said, this work seeks to contribute to a discourse on the liberation of gender, sexuality and even race from the vestiges of white supremacy. For those who long for a different imagination of human identity and dignity I humbly submit that this text might be considered a supporting element within a strategy towards the liberation from the rhetorics, the discourse and the supporting knowledge base which maintains the various interlocking oppressions.

I find myself to be somewhat of a prophet simply because I advocate for sustainability and authenticity among communities of people whom I actually feel, could really care less about either of them, particularly regarding gender and sexuality, unless it betrays normative frameworks grounded in those interlocking oppressions. Those who accept and even embrace, for a lesser profit, a reality conjured by and for white supremacy. Then there are those who have been lulled to sleep falling victim to the strategies of capitalism. This text seeks as its primary calling to wake up those masses of people who long for liberation. Its core grace is to make space; to make a way so that the authentic lines of liberation might emerge bringing forth a sacred and holy sanctuary for the heart. And isn't this what the struggle for gender, sexuality, racial, economic and political liberation has been about, a space for the heart to be?

It is hoped that, after reading this text, the reader is moved, even compelled to live out their liberation; to come out of the proverbial closet and to be authentic and thus disempower the vestiges of white supremacy. Coming out is challenging and courageous and at times sacrificial, moving those who encounter the one coming out to a new space of consciousness. Now while coming out has been about gender and sexuality identity, —proxies for real and deeper issues—I suggest that it goes far beyond the physical to the mental, emotional and the spiritual. Beloved, the call of life is a call to liberation and this has always been the sacred narrative of humanity and this text calls the reader to recognize this indispensable truth of human existence.

The task of living out our liberation is not easy, but easy is not the point of life, or manageability. Life is about the heart and soul, revealing for me, questions such as, "How do we make a difference while we are in the land of the living? What is our legacy, not in the sense of a narrative oriented towards white supremacy, but in our authentic presence? This text does not emerge out of some fantasy or naiveté but out of a hard core engagement of life, love and liberation.

Acknowledgements

On a journey called life, God instills a great mystical love seldom understood yet so very present. Self-discovery, hope and a compelling need to "be" emerge as a provocative narrative of that mystical love and of a life called forth long ago. Each relationship on the journey embodies questions of curiosity, frustrations, disappointments, meaning, pain, sorrow, joy, mistakes, forgiveness, and reconciliation, all grounded in a deep-seeded mercy and bathed in a great light of grace as only God would intend. At times choices made only reveal a vision before rooted in divine intent and imagination.

There are many people involved in God's plan for us, each contributing, sometimes unaware, ingredients necessary to unveil the hand of God. This book emerges as such. I am thankful to my mother, Rosemaryand my sister, Yolanda. The City of Refuge, United Church of Christ, Professors Ibrahim Farajaje and Gabriella Lettini of Starr King School for the Ministry, Tapestry Ministries and First Christian Church of Oakland Christian Church Disciples of Christ for their sense of divine witness as this book was being lived in real time.

Beloved, the process of change and transformation can be a most intimate and dynamic affair, seldom understood and mind-blowing, yet a most constant presence. Much patience and love are required so that the divine work of life will manifest. This book is also the fruit of a most intimate and sacred relationship with my spiritual parents Jonathon and Trippta.

Chapter 1

Introduction

"You are evil, just plain evil."
This was a statement made to me by a black woman I encountered at a local grocery store in Norfolk, Virginia. Her statement reminded me of my conservative theological stances on gender and sexuality prior to my own experience of *Coming Out* as a Black/African-American transgender woman. I remember at that moment asking myself, "Where did this statement come from?" I actually had a pretty good idea what she meant. I had been a minister at a conservative church, with a conservative theology. I had preached a conservative message, even attended Regent University, a conservative university founded by conservative icon Pat Robertson, where issues and concerns of diversity regarding gender and sexuality outside of the normative binary construction of male and female preferably with the ability to give birth, were considered an abomination and a pastoral care concern.

Her statement has been with me since that day and becomes the ground of my longing to address gender and sexual identity and a compelling reason for this work. The thesis of this work is the presence of the divine black transgender feminine, i.e. Monica Joy, which emerges as the divine transgender feminine and the sacred black masculine, i.e. Alexander, considered a social and cultural production of the black experience in the United States,

1

are interpreted as equitable identities embodied within the human body, considered in this text a queer space of fluidity, and a representation of the infinite. Monica and Alexander are not evil but simply represent a different albeit a more diverse ontological presence of gender and sexual identity with implications towards a particular evolution of being. What I mean here is that they represent a continuous unveiling of who I am, intellectually, emotionally, spiritually and physically. In some sense, who I am is an ongoing discourse of spirit and soul possession, becoming more and more evident as I interrogate ideas and concepts of gender and sexual identity beyond the normative modes of being, experienced here as an act of spiritual/religious decolonization.

Similar to Mama Lola, in Karen McCarthy Brown's book, Mama Lola[1], I find myself to be a vessel of complex spiritual intent grounded in notions of the African ancestors. Similar to Mama Lola's female spirit group called Ezili which consists of Freda and Danto, Monica Joy and Alexander exist in tension, unable to entirely vanquish the other, both presenting particular circumstances and desires as each has a different narrative. In the tension between Monica Joy and Alexander, the "soul and spirit" explore questions of race, sexuality, economics, class and gender, and the intersectionality of oppression. Monica Joy is a black transgender woman, tall, attractive, bisexual, spiritual, a minister, healer and visionary. She is prophetic, a prayer warrior, meditative, and in conversation with the divine. She lives and breathes her faith, queering what it means to be feminine and masculine in the African/Black American context. She is courageous, always in danger.

Alexander is a quiet black man, a construction of society and culture, somewhat safer in comparison. He is an intellectual and a quiet storm. He is tall, dark and handsome and heterosexual. He can be a man's man intent on getting what he needs when he needs it. He too is full of faith, spiritual and a prayer warrior. He is the antithesis of a white supremacy that would put him in prison given the chance. So, he too is in danger. Both identities exhibit notions of mysticism and the ecstatic, embracing a particular negation of

1. Brown, *Mama Lola*, 256–257.

ontological colonization, as inferred by Franz Fanon's Black Skin, White Masks, and the acceptance of the infinite. Monica Joy and Alexander require space, both spiritual and physical and, in this, both are compelling vessels of a persistent sacred witness of the in-breaking of the infinite. At times this is very frustrating, simply because of the need for the people encountered to locate the body, as indoctrinated by institutions grounded in white supremacy and its privilege, in a specific binary category; not possessing the language or the imagination necessary to respect the soul and spirit's particular expression, which in my case denotes queer/transgender. My impression is that they have an irrational need for gender security, to make the body and its presentation fit into male or female, with no alternative possibility.

"When [they] meet someone whose [gender] identity is unclear, that throws [their] own identity into flux.

—ALICE DOMURAT DREGER, BIOETHICS PROFESSOR[2]"

It is within this context that the soul and spirit evolve. Monica Joy and Alexander present a particular ethical imperative as each queers the expectations of race, gender and sexuality, eliciting the rhetorical wrath of people who embrace a different world view. That said, my journey, my struggle within in the cultural, historical and religious milieu of the U.S., is what Cornel West entitles *"Subversive Joy and Revolutionary Patience in Black Christianity"* in his treatment of the tragic elements in Afro-American Christianity.[3]

Far from the staid sensibilities of the Black Church and its norms of civility and decency procured on the plantation[4] the proposal of Jesus Christ, the divine and the sacred of Christianity, at least in this writer's experience is indecent, obscene and at

2. Abraham. *She's All That. Interview with WNBA player Brittney Griner November issue of Elle,* 310.

3. West, *Prophetic Fragments,* 161–165.

4. Brooten, Beyond Slavery, Overcoming its Religious and Sexual Legacies, 1–7.

times homeless, and thus far more in touch with the human condition. The use of the terms divine and sacred within a discourse on the human condition are a means to reflect the criticality of an authentic voice of the infinite. The use of the term "infinite" in this project denotes all that is beyond human interpretations and constructions yet inclusive of the same. It is measureless and indefinable, yet intimate to every facet of a dynamic life. It is sacred and mystical; birthing all that is into human and cosmic consciousness. In contrast the identifying term, "God," from an historical perspective must be considered a colonizing identity. Loaded with particular images it promotes concepts and ideas of nationalism which is not the point of this project.

That said, working on this project I seek to be authentic and concise as an expression within the art of queer hospitality. Queer hospitality is the art of welcoming the stranger and their difference as a signifier of an intimacy of the infinite. For the one sensitive to the infinite, hospitality is a means to acknowledge that love, like life itself, emerges from the infinite, even the everlasting into the heart and soul of all that is. This project is also an invitation into a life emerging from and immersed in the infinite and daily engaging in social, cultural and economic constructions.

I seek to make these matters of the soul understandable, and accessible, to reveal the roots of a liberating consciousness. There is realization that this work has historical significance with implications towards the liberation of the human soul from those systems and structures that sequester human experience. It is an appeal to be very attentive, on the part of the writer and the reader, as this is one of the rarest forms of love. What I mean is, there is a "spiritual gravity"[5] to this project and this must be the reality which undergirds the whole matter.

This project is also an appeal to those Mystical, Pagan, Wiccan, Islam, Indigenous Shaman and Voodou influences which are significant spiritual markers on a path of a revelation of being. From my first therapy session through a dark night of the soul in Norfolk, Virginia, to my engagement of Shamanism beginning

---

5. Springsted, *Simone Weil and the Suffering of Love*, 57.

with a shaman at a Memphis Tennessee Greyhound bus station to an encounter with Voodou, my life has been about a revelation of being. The implications of a revelation of being are an increasing cognizance of the spirit world and its participation in temporal life as well as an increased embrace of my agency and escape from ideas and notions of colonization.

A revelation of being requires strategies of survival as I encounter people who would seek to end my life. As such, these spiritual traditions become a primary support system of my liberation from colonized notions of gender and sexuality. There *are* aspects of this journey that are simply a vision lived out and this, not of my own choosing, a journey from the head to the heart, from the philosophical to an earthiness. It has been a prophetic mystical path. Dynamic, terrifying and intense yet full of a steadfast hope. Life, for me, is revealed as a meditation of the infinite as I encounter the gravity of this hope, contained in my struggle for liberation from colonization, white supremacy and their interpretations and terminologies that daily seek to enslave love and even imagination itself.

Particularly as a minister ordained in the Christian tradition who lives on the edge of the margins, identifying as an African-American/Black transgender woman, I find that culture and faith in the U.S are still, even today, to a large extent, narrowly defined by what I consider oppressive interpretations for the sake of race, sex and gender privilege.[6] These interpretations; the basis of relational empowerment, as well as common space impacting various facets of political and socio-cultural and economic life, seemingly for some, are the only legitimate religious tradition.

In an article in *The Root*, an online news magazine which focuses on socio-political discourse in the African-American/Black community, Jenée Desmond, wrote an article entitled, *Please Stop Assuming all Blacks are Christian, Race Manners: The good news about being an atheist who's annoyed by this stereotype is that you're*

6.. Colombo, Cullen, Lisle, eds. What Price Independence? Social Reactions to Lesbians, Spinsters, Widows and Nuns, 257–259.

not alone.[7] She writes of a particular narrative, which holds that a significant majority of African Americans identify as Christian and that to be any other spiritual/religious tradition somehow denies some type of salvific privilege embodied in the black experience in America. That the only legitimate faith tradition for the black person is Christianity learned and embraced on the plantation, necessarily grounded in the master-slave paradigm. The challenge for me then was to move from this paradigm, to expand my consciousness, to know the divine infinite beyond any particular oppression.

What I mean is that life is a spiritual autobiography of the divine infinite, calling forth attentiveness to the moment. In a world where notions of contextualities and containers rule the day, I want to suggest that a thought of the infinite might be too abstract for some yet to embrace life, even action from the perspective of a container or simply as a matter of limitation becomes a necessary discourse on oppression for the sake of some integrity of that container. Racism, sexism, economics, even the cross, become oppressive structures for the maintenance of the integrity of scarcity and limitation.

As I write and rewrite these words, I reflect upon the numerous wars and murders that occur because of some so-called integrity of scarcity and limitation in regard to gender and sexuality. In this sense I am reminded of the Global War on non-normative Gender and Sexual identity. I think about the criminalization of my humanity for the sake of some racial patriarchal heterosexual sensibility, in essence, sequestering my experience with God. While particular advances have been made regarding gender and sexuality there are still laws which criminalize my body. I find myself wondering why laws and regulations are needed if being "straight" is an authentic space of being, since the authentic requires no law or rule. On a recent radio report on National Public Radio (NPR)[8] a woman who identifies as a lesbian spoke of the injustices aimed

---

7. Desmond. *Please stop Assuming all Blacks are Christian, Race Manners: The good news about being an atheist who's annoyed by this stereotype is that you're not alone.* (The Root)

8. National Public Radio story 1/8/2014.

at the LGBTQ community in Russia under Vladimir Putin and the Russian Orthodox Church. Clearly, injustice in Putin's Russia only counts if your humanity fits within the limited capacity of his and the Russian Orthodox Church's imagination. And then there are the laws in Uganda prohibiting homosexual relations and condemning any witness to prison.

This mindset is no different than that of Stalin, Hitler, the Ku Klux Klan, Idi Amin Dada or any person who embraces a life of hatred and discontent. I think for some, hatred has become an interpretation of a type of cultural and societal imperative for the sake of the heteronormative binary. In contrast to the in humanity and a lack of imagination of Putin and his Russia, I experience life as a movement with an everincreasing enlightenment of mystical proportions revealing pathologies of contextualism and/or containerism. What I mean here is that my own spiritual transformation has revealed that the incessant need to respect the limits of human understanding has become the cause, even the reason for the very oppressions that seek to deny the divinity of difference. I think at some point I long for notions of the preenlightenment, even with its human conditions, when difference was interpreted by many as sacred and authentic, even divine. This longing has led me to embrace a process of negation to somehow cope with God's difference within me.

The necessity of negation becomes apparent as I seek to (1) attain some consciousness of the layers of colonization and the need to decolonize and (2) to develop a different frame of reference regarding what t means to be legitimate. Emerging out of a process of negation, and apophatic ethical realism, my journey of gender and sexual identity represents an alignment with the interests of Mother Earth as the embodiment of the cosmic deity. According to Roland Faber, author of *Bodies of the Void: Polyphilia and Theoplicity* in the book *Apophatic Bodies*, "Negation is a position of "unbounding," of "de-limiting," in proposing that the deity is in its "essence" un-bound and in-finite."[9]

---

9. Faber, *Bodies of the Void: Polyphilia and Theoplicity* in Apophatic Bodies, 201.

Apophatic ethical realism emerges out of my readings of Emmanuel Levinas' concepts on infinity and his retrieval of the" apophatic tradition in pre-modern epistemology."[10] A reading of Levinas suggests that God transcends all that is known and unknown yet is intimate with all that is.[11] "The demand of the other issues from an unknown God who loves the stranger."[12] The ethical, of which I read Levinas, becomes an imperative of the intimate, and this emerging as a response to infinity. It is an appeal to the thoughts of Mevlana Jalaluddin Rumi (1207–1273) and his mystical ecstasy of the divine infinite.[13]

There are four goals for this project. The first goal is to begin a discourse on the Coming Out of the divine black transgender feminine and the sacred black masculine as equitable and integrated identities embodied within a body. A corollary of a discussion on gender is addressing the place of black masculinities within a fluid identity and delinking the whole structure of gender from white desire. The second goal is to present the body as that luminal space of cosmic ecstasy, a queer space of inspiration and liberation for the revelation of spiritual intent. A third goal, and possibly the most urgent, is an engagement of the framework that undergirds the present situation. It is about the present knowledge base that supports and gives language to the interlocking oppressions of American society and culture. A fourth goal is the locating of the divine black transgender feminine and the sacred black masculine in a queer post-colonial architecture.

CONSIDERATIONS OF METHOD AND ANALYSIS

The method deployed in addressing the liberation of the divine black transgender feminine and the sacred black masculine is a method that seeks to delink gender, sexuality and race from those

10. Levinas. Alterity and Transcendance

11. Wyschogrod. *Emmanuel Levinas, The Problem of Ethical Metaphysics*, xi.

12. Ibid.

13. www.khamuch.com accessed September 15, 2013.

structures, i.e. rhetorical as well as philosophical from white desire and privilege. I write as one whose cultural and social narrative reflects the historical realities of a southern *slaveocracy* and Franz Fanon's white gaze. Living daily in the academy and in the media, both which I consider forms of Fanon's white gaze, impress upon me first as an academic and a transgender scholar and then as a person of African descent that in certain corporate, political, economic and religious circles "whiteness" still denotes legitimacy; it still rules the day. The current political environment demonstrably exhibits this through rhetorical strategies that call into question the legitimacy of the first president who identifies as African-American and issues and concerns of immigration which supposedly challenge the supremacy of white sensibilities.

The vitriolic language has been profound, revealing the deep fissures of racial, ethnic and gender impropriety that have lit the fires of secession. The delinking of legitimacy from white sensibilities and desires necessarily opens possibilities of a critique of modernity, post-modernity, rationality and knowledge. At this point I will take the opportunity to define my argument for delinking legitimacy from white sensibility and desire. According to Walter D. Mignolo, author of *Delinking, the rhetoric of modernity, the logic of coloniality and the grammar of decolonality,* delinking means to change the terms and not just the content of the conversation—the content has been changed, in the modern/colonial world by Christianity (e.g. theology of liberation); by liberalism (e.g. the U.S. support of de-colonization in Africa and Asia during the Cold War) and by Marxism (also supporting de-colonization of Africa and Asia during the Cold War).[14]

One of the goals of this project is to shift the discourse on legitimacy from appeasing white desire, whether corporate or societal imagination, to a different narrative space where legitimacy becomes located in critical difference. Critical difference in the context of this project, in contrast to critical sameness, is a means to embrace the sacredness and holiness of difference. It becomes a

---

14. Mignolo. *Delinking, The rhetoric of modernity, the logic of coloniality and the grammar of de-coloniality,* 459.

means by which to appreciate the divine in all people and as such to experience the infinite and thus liberation. Difference denotes a representation of the sacred, even the profane. In contrast, critical sameness, which I suggest conjures up images of "a bride in waiting" referring to a particular antiquated Christian notion of salvation and the return of Jesus Christ, undergirds many cultural and societal structures, is a means to develop the other and marginalize them to a point where whatever divinity, holiness or sacredness exists, is questioned.

I am cognizant that sameness as a narrative structure of identification within notions of white supremacy still pervades the common thought of many. It's like people feed off of sameness and this as a psychological imperative, that they are secure if the people around them look or act like them, that there is a common order to identity. I remember being told by a friend who is a pastor that "they aren't ready for you. You are too different."

You may ask, "Why do I use critical difference instead of diversity?" I think for me there must be a complete divorce in all ways from anything that reflects the white narrative of desire or anything that somehow denotes strategies of whiteness to maintain power over. As such there must be a question of epistemological origin and the attending reason. After living as an African-American transgender woman who is queer and as an African-American man I am impressed that I have a different narrative scheme which emerges out of my social location, thus my social location informs my lens of social interaction. This is significant particularly because of the marginal status of the two identities as criminalized bodies.

As a black male body I am grounded in the lives of Rodney King, Oscar Grant, Howard Thurman, Martin Luther King, Jr., Malcolm X, and memories of the Lynching Tree. That said, identifying as an African-American male in a racist patriarchal society protected and affirmed as a matter and concern of law enforcement I present a particular fear to those averse to critical difference. As such, I experience the gaze, the stare, the turning away of people who walk into my presence, continually under suspicion by a culture and society that encounters me as the antithesis of white supremacy. I live out a narrative of incarceration, historical institutional injustice, continually suspect by a society and culture that identifies me as a criminal body. I remember when I would go to the store I would notice the reaction of people, the stance of police, even women clutching tightly to their purses. I had read about this cultural dynamic but since living my life as transgender and queer I am very much aware of the disparities. It is in this context that I remember the incarceration of many black men and boys.

In 2009 I had the opportunity to visit congressional offices to lobby for the passage of the hate crimes bill. While my delegation was received enthusiastically, we were told that some African-American clergy were also lobbying against the hate crimes bill. Unfortunately, like James Baldwin, I find that some in the African-American community, for all of the oppression which they have experienced, can be the greatest expression of oppression particularly on matters of gender and sexuality. I fear that the plantation mentality instilled by the slave owner still stubbornly persists in some corners. .

The analysis addresses an historical, systemic marginalization of the color of my skin, and my transgression of an accepted gender construct. It presents a sense of uniqueness, a sacredness, yet is tempered by the realities which call forth the Transgender Day of Remembrance. At this juncture of the project a discussion on the concept of liberation in regards to gender identity in the American context calls for a definition of certain terms that might be considered pivotal in the development of this project.

Defining terms represents an understanding of the epistemology that undergirds various discourses that support cultural frameworks of gender identity. I suggest here that the field of epistemology which is concerned with propositional knowledge, that is, knowledge that such-and-such is true, rather than other forms of knowledge; for example, knowledge how to such-and-such[15] is important as the ground in developing a liberative discourse on gender identity. Epistemology raises a question about the location

15. Routledge Encyclopedia of Philosophy.

of agency and the interpretation of experience. According to Judith Butler, author of the book *Gender Trouble*, "the question of locating 'agency' usually associated with the viability of the 'subject' is understood to have some stable bodies of the existence prior to the cultural field that it negotiates. Or, if the subject is culturally constructed, it is nevertheless vested with an agency, usually figured as the capacity for reflexive mediation that remains intact regardless of its cultural embeddedness."[16]

Coming Out then in the context of this project on gender identity addresses a narrow mindset which emerges out of a colonial regime, the ground of American/U.S. cultural discourse. It is about coming out of a master-slave narrative pathology which assumes legitimacy of gender and sexuality; heteronormative concerns of industry and state, as production oriented, consequently raping their humanity and rejecting their divinity, seeking to recalibrate notions of materialism and the incarnation. While this project is oriented towards cultural historical scholarship it, by necessity, engages significant theological points of reflection, albeit from a *queer* perspective.

The term queer, as understood in this project, denote one's difference, strangeness' positively.[17] To accept and embrace oneself for what and who they are regardless of the cultural or social regime. A queer perspective emerges as a liberation of mind, body and soul necessarily raising critique of various social constructions. The implications of queer are a deconstruction of those constructs which form the basis as well as characterize those interlocking oppressions.

My journey thus far I find that I must view this path as queer. It is a crooked path through theological terrains of conservative, centrist and progressive, from the Bible Belt of Virginia to the liberal crucible of the San Francisco Bay area. I experience each of these terrains as a location of theological polarization with implications towards social, cultural and political discourse. Theological polarization results when communities of faith interpret a sacred

16. Butler. *Gender Trouble*, 195.
17. Sullivan. *A Critical Introduction to Queer Theory*, 1.

text from different points on the continuum of faith, making their particular interpretation the absolute embodiment of divinity. I lift up out of these terrains God's curriculum of grace for the path. Grace, mercy and even the Cross become unwilling agents of those interlocking oppressions. I remember being invited to a church in Norfolk, Virginia by a good friend and mentor. Of course, being in Virginia I was skeptical but he said that the United Church of Christ had endorsed transgender people of faith and that my presence in that church would be good. Well, my very presence actually caused serious commotion. One lady left the church after fifty years as a member. The pastor, when asked about the situation said, "I am the first female pastor of this church." Seemingly, even though the congregation, which was primarily African-American, embraced grace, mercy and the cross those very same images were used to oppress the stranger, to reject hospitality and at least for me a divine presence.

Divine presence, i.e. queer in the context of this project, is rooted in a lived experience and grounded in an uncommon faith that emerges out of generations of people who fought and died in and for the struggle of liberation, to experience their sense of divine presence. Queer lifts up, out of the cultural and social milieu, sites that are spaces of contestation. Judith Butler, in her book *Bodies that Matter*[18] writes, "If the term "queer" is to be a site of collective contestation, the point of departure for a set of historical reflections and future imaginings, it will have to remain that which is, in the present, never fully owned, but always and only redeployed, twisted, queered from a prior usage. This also means that it will doubtless have to be yielded in favor of terms that do the political work more effectively. Such a yielding may well become necessary in order to accommodate, without domesticating, democratizing contestations that have and will redraw the contours of the movement, ways that can never be fully anticipated in advance."[19]

From a progressive cultural-historical-theological perspective, living queer signifies that my existence emanates from an

---

18. Butler. *Bodies that Matter*, 228.

19. Butler, *Bodies that Matter*, 228.

expansive divine imagination necessarily challenging the normative common imagination of gender identity. Living queer is a
difficult and albeit challenging calling that critiques societal and
cultural norms and myths of hetero-industrialized productions
of gender identity necessarily creating different possibilities for
transformation.

Queer is sacred, as praxis and performance, and emerges
with political presence. The politics of presence being the very
real impact of queer on the political schema, as the realization
of a liberative society rises out of a political wellspring of justice
grounded in the real lives and experiences of people living queer.
That said, queer, at least in my life, unleashes a revelation of the
spectrums of gender and sexual fluidity and the ensuing tensions
that accompany these realities within a hetero-normative culture.
This is profoundly difficult and challenging. How do I deal with
this situation? I must reflect on my situation as one who is from
James Baldwin's "*Another Country*"[20], checking my passport of
performance and praxis with a riveting intensity. I must gain some
understanding of the depth of this experience.

Out of this reflection on life the divine black transgender
feminine emerges as a cosmic discourse characterized as the Holy
Obscene. It is provocative and indecent, liberating and thus revealing a different imagination of the divine to humanity, necessarily
critiquing a binary oriented culture and society. On the other hand
the sacred black masculine is the eroticism of God and is the initial
creative and intimate force of God. Eroticism is the life force that
compels the dynamism of creation. According to Dwight N. Hopkins, in *The Construction of the Black Male Body in Sexuality and
the Sacred*, eroticism speaks to black men's identity flooded with
a life force in their very bodies.[21] For Hopkins, eroticism is the
sacred spark of creation and the ultimate state of consciousness.

20. Baldwin. Another Country

21. Hopkins. The Construction of the Black Male Body in Sexuality and
the Sacred, Sources for the Theological Reflection eds. Ellison and Douglas,
213.

The obscene and the eroticism then are revealed as the narrative of God.

Gender identity presents a narrative of life as a discourse of cosmic, divine origin and of critical difference. The feminine and masculine, which Monica Joy and Alexander represent, are transformational in orientation and oppositional in their strategies towards the cultural and historical religious binary oriented structures which have undergirded occidental discourses on gender and sexual identity. Current notions of gender and sexual identity are based primarily in the narrative of racial patriarchy. As such, the practices, performances and rituals are oppressive, demanding that culture adhere to a particular type and degree of practice and performance resulting in a profound human tragedy. That said, a different notion of gender and sexual identity becomes the good news by providing an avenue of liberation for the divine black transgender feminine and the sacred black masculine from the interlinking structures of racial patriarchal domination.

This work is a rallying cry for healing from the idolatry of heteronormativity perpetrated on humanity by a culture and society characterized by the interlocking systems of oppression that dominate and sequester authentic human experience. Human experience as pertains to gender and sexual identity has been made to be a tool of mediation for the production and consumption of normative culture. As such, it is experienced as consumption-oriented, a social construction considered here of a compromised position for economic, political and social import.

My search for an authentic sense of gender and sexual identity is a primary feature of my life's work. The truth of my life experience is living beyond binary notions of gender and sexual identity as who I am emerges from the infinite. Living the consequences and the implications of who I am, I must take solace from the life of James Baldwin, a scholar and writer, a man of critical difference as he too wrestled with self-discovery and self-knowledge, seeking some relief but to no avail.[22] I struggle with the ethics of gender and sexual identity, i.e. concerns of appreciation for my own mul-

22. Baldwin. *Another Country.*

tiplicity of genders, i.e. feminine, masculine and the "in-between," accountability and moral agency within intimacy, the community of faith and a broader society that is physically, rhetorically and politically subservient towards desires of hetero-normalcy.

My presence in social and cultural strata, which at times contest who I am, even my calling of God, has made me cognizant that the structure of gender and sexual identity and its subservience to systems of reason and profit exists because of a pathology, which I suggest here is rooted in the plantation system. The use of the term plantation system in this thesis denotes the colonization, enslavement and industrialization of gender and sexuality formed in the context of the master-slave narrative, which has historically undergirded modes of capitalism from the beginnings of the Republic. In this context matters of self-discovery are experienced as hostages of this pathology and the associated interlocking oppressions that support the overall socio-economic program.

Self-discovery, in the midst of entrenched plantation system pathology, becomes a monumental task summoning every God-given grace. In this sense, gender, sexuality and race must be considered historical categories for the production of oppression. In contrast, self-discovery receives gender, sexuality and race as a means towards divine intent, a mystical quest. Self-discovery is an opportunity to engage liberation and transformation to reconceptualize the uniquely American constructs of gender, sexuality, and race and their various frameworks. My journey of self-discovery has been counter-cultural, difficult, and fraught with complications and setbacks, consequential of violating the limits established to sequester the human imagination.

As I travel this road of self-discovery, a persistent question arises, "Who or what does gender, sexuality and race appeal to?" The issue of appeal stands front and center particularly as it relates to the concern of passing for the transgender person, or hiding or not hiding in plain sight. Those who do pass reap the rewards and benefits of heteronormative idolatry and those who do not pass, lacking the support—whether financial, spiritual, or racial

—face the violence of that idolatry, some giving their last to be themselves.

At points, writing becomes a burden as it rekindles memories of incidents involving the death of several of my black transgender brothers and sisters in Norfolk, Virginia, their only *"crime"* being a different sense of being which jeopardized normative notions of gender and sexual identity, provoking an already violent culture towards more physical, emotional and spiritual violence. The police, the protectors and defenders of heteronormativity, necessarily put a low priority on their murders because they were considered to be immoral and evil by certain religious and political groups in the community. Religion, politics and media presented gender and sexuality as highly subjugated states of being regulated by church and state, imposed through cultural, social and religious rhetoric unleashing images of the Southern plantation slaveocracy. Violence erupts as the transgender person reveals the fallacy of the regulatory regime.

Today my community of faith is celebrating the Transgender Day of Remembrance. Each year we celebrate the memory of transgender people from around the world who have given their last to live out their authenticity, their divinity. They have now become that silent witness to a war that has raged against transgender people and anyone who does not fit into the fine lines of the binary structure of hetero-normativity. Tragically, as I was walking down a street in San Francisco, I was verbally accosted by young men who called me a plethora of derogatory names and then one said that he would put a gun to my head and blow it off. So, not much has changed beyond the political rhetoric of policy making.

Seemingly, there is an embodiment of hatred towards the transgender person by some people so deep that the evil which undergirds that hatred becomes palpable even to the touch. I will now expand this discourse on gender and sexuality to include a discussion on the sacred black masculine.

SACRED BLACK MASCULINITIES, A DIFFERENT MORAL VISION BEYOND THE NORMATIVE DISCOURSE OF RACE, GENDER AND SEXUALITY

From the outset, a discussion on the sacred black masculine emerges out of challenging, impassioned conversations with friends and colleagues around the oppressions encountered by black men. As noted by Robert Staples in his book *Black Masculinity, the Black Male's Role in American Society*, "it is difficult to think of a more controversial role in American society than the black male."[23] In her book, *We Real Cool, Black Men and Masculinity*, Bell Hooks writes, "By writing this book I wanted to challenge the misguided notion that ours is a culture that loves black men. I wanted to make it clear that there is a crisis in the black male spirit in our nation. And that crisis is not because black men are an endangered species, rather it is a crisis perpetuated by widespread dehumanization, by the continued placement of black males outside of humanity."[24]

Similar to the divine transgender feminine, sacred black masculinities challenge the narcissistic tendencies of a totalitarian state and are, as a consequence, controversial. Both represent an evolution of sorts, opening and broadening a discourse on the accessibility of race, gender, class and sexuality. That said, I did not want to dilute a discussion of the divine black transgender feminine, or develop a narrative where the two were in competition with each other. Also needing to employ a critical lens to sacred black masculinities, particularly as a context within the artful strategy of cultural and civil warfare, I sought only to deal with the divine black transgender feminine yet as an actual reality within a lived experience, not to include it as a part of an ontological discussion, however risky, at least in this writer's mind, denies the prophetic and mystical wisdom encountered in the presence and reality of the sacred black masculine, hence the usage of the term queer.

That said, I must frame the topic of sacred black masculinities as their own theological and ontological discourse and not a

---

23. Staples. *The Black Male's Role in American Society*, 1.
24. Hooks. *We Real Cool, Black Men and Masculinity*, 134.

reaction or response to the established norm or even a transgender sub-discourse. Identity, at least to a writer born and raised in South Central Los Angeles in the 1960's, at the height of the Black Power and Civil Rights movements, is not about an identity defined and approved by the norms of corporate, political or religious regimes but about a sacred, authentic presence with a different moral vision and authority with historical implications. This becomes the ground of a treatment of sacred black masculinities.

There is a peculiar holiness and communal presence that defines the sanctity of black masculinities within the African Diaspora narrative yet this communal presence is also a significant dilemma for a Black Man[25] in a context compelled under duress, by a structure rooted in colonization and the lynching tree, which has historically situated black masculinities on the margins of white supremacy. Significant systemic oppressions, strategically embodied in the structures of normative politics, economics, education, employment and income, i.e., the student track to the prison industrial complex, food canyons, and drug policies which reflect the racist tendencies of the U.S. legal system which engages sacred black masculinities as subordinate subversive identities as maintained through a corporate media complex and a politics codified through a legal system that frames black masculinities as guilty as charged upon arrival at birth.[26]

This situation of sacred black masculinities, as evidenced in the death of Trayvon Martin, a young black teen in Florida who was killed at the hands of a man named George Zimmerman, a White-Hispanic man, who profiled him as a threat while he was coming from the corner store in his neighborhood with Skittles and iced tea, presents black masculinities as a necessary discourse on the strategies of survival and existence of the sacred black masculinities, combating self-hatred and the paradigm of the runaway slave.

25. Staples. *Black Masculinity, The Black Male's Role in American Society,* 7.

26. Waters. A Desired Eulogy: For Emmett, Virgil, Trayvon, and Jordan article in Huffington Post accessed February 15, 2014.

The election of the first president of African descent should not be considered a means by which to endorse the so-called reform of white supremacy; that the purveyors of the normative structure have been overcome, but a strategy towards the recognition of the struggles of the black man in America, even as the advocates for white supremacy and "white liberation" double down as a matter of racial trauma. Transitions *are* traumatic experiences especially when they shake the foundations of traditional so-called rational paradigms. I recently went to a gun manufacturer's website to do some research on gun violence and discovered that gun sales had gone through the roof when President Barack Obama won reelection.

The election of 2012, even more so than the election of 2008, exemplifies the mental state of race and power relations in the United States. My God, the formerly enslaved have run amuck, they have lost their way and their position in the social and culture order. The existence of the black man is an antithetical presence in a society grounded in white supremacy is real, a knowledge fully embraced within a common narrative of American society.

That said, a treatment of sacred black masculinities is necessary because in a real sense the black man is one of the least appreciated, in the context of U.S. racial patriarchy. Considered a threat, sacred black masculinities as a whole, historically, have been a great act of hope and support of U. S. racial patriarchy. So, the black man must be considered the hope as well as the threat to a structure and its interlocking oppressions which denies his legitimacy and, in this sense, humanity at all levels of racial patriarchy. This sets up the black man for various forms and processes of marginalization which are meant to assist in the maintenance of a structure created and developed and maintainedby and for the white European colonizer.

Sacred black masculinities have significant stratifications and intersections of oppressions to work through which have been developed specifically for them. This is primarily because white supremacy considers sacred black masculinities to be a primary threat to its totalitarian regime. Clearly the sacred and the truth must be separated from the myth established to support the interests of white supremacy. I suggest here that this is one reason why most of the black militant/intelligencia were slaughtered both physically and politically in the 1960's and a reason today why the music industry –– hip-hop in particular –– spew lyrics that maintain the dehumanization of those sacred black masculinities, the black feminist/womanist and their community as a whole. This is a strategy produced in concert with programs such as "Stand Your ground" in Florida and "Stop and Frisk" in New York City which maintain a myth first imposed by the plantation owners in the days of southern slaveocracy.

No secret here that a concerted effort, structured and strategized through various racist/sexist frameworks, oriented hyper-myths, on the part of the U.S. government, the corporate community, media complex and their agents continue to marginalize any stirrings of Black Power and black men simply because the only authorized power in the U.S. was and still is white supremacy, even in its so-called social and political diversity and inclusion in a mindset of whiteness.[27] This is also a reason for various political discourses on poverty, education, HIV/Aids, economy and the Affordable Care Act (ACA) or Obamacare to become proxies for a civil war. Reflecting on this unfortunate circumstance I find that sacred black masculinities *can* present a different moral vision of humanity. Even with the layers and layers of oppression meant to marginalize, even destroy their humanity overall, sacred black masculinities have been able to survive, overcome, and even thrive within those interlocking oppressions.

Sacred black masculinities have been that critical difference causing their nemesis to reckon with their totalitarian colonial ambitions of patriarchy and historical discourses on racial superiority. Most notably this has been evidenced in black men such as President Barack Obama, Rev. Dr. Martin Luther King, Jr., Rev. Dr. Jeremiah Wright, Malcolm X, General Colin Powell, Senator Corey Booker, 100 Black Men community activist Bayard Rustin,

27. Hooks. *Don't Make me hurt you, Black male violence in We Real Cool, Black Men and Masculinity*, 44–66.

professors Cornel West and Michael Eric Dyson. These black men and their particular masculinities, and many like them not mentioned here, represent a different moral vision, one very much influenced by the black experience in diaspora, yet able to mediate their particular masculinity with a structure that was not developed or created to reflect their vision of the masculine.

As evidenced by their reaction to the election of Barack Obama, the first president of African decent, these men represent a clear and present danger to the ideas of the totalitarian regime. In a weird sense these black men, and others like them, become a compelling reason for white supremacy to invest in a prison industrial complex. Surviving in a context of racial patriarchy, the black man must focus on building movements of sustainability, i.e. movements that change the racial and economic terrain imposed as a matter of collective privilege and power. The black man, cognizant of the unfortunate situation, must see and experience their particular sacred black masculinity as transformative within the culture and society through the creation and development of ideas which emerge out of their collective experiences.

I suggest here that as the black man experiences *his* sacred masculinity as the critical difference, he will gradually shift a narrative which has been ingrained by the oppressor and will liberate his mind regarding more diverse genders and sexualities even within the black community. That said, sacred black masculinities are called, in concert with the divine black transgender feminine, to make a space for a new and different space of gender, sexual and racial legitimacy. I suggest that the ground of this new legitimacy should be a ground that reflects notions of a post-colonial imagination, which the black man from the imagination of white supremacy and its desire and by definition racial patriarchy. What I mean here is that the black man must create and develop his own space of being, even his own legitimacy, they must be their social revolution. This requires what Kwame Nkrumah, one of Africa's most renowned philosophers and political leaders calls an intellectual revolution. He writes, in his book *Consciencism, Philosophy and Ideology for De-Colonization and Development* with particular reference to the African Revolution, "Social Revolution must have, standing firmly behind it, an intellectual revolution in which our thinking and philosophy are directed at the redemption of our society."[28] Decolonization of sacred black masculinities must have as their primary purpose the decolonization of the black mind.

Sacred black masculinities, based on the words of Kwame Nkrumah become a hopeful discourse within a post-colonial narrative as they create new and different self-concepts through embracing their authenticity. To once again embrace their authenticity, even their divinity they must dare to decolonize the mind.[29] Rejecting normative racial, gender and sexual discourses, they accept and embrace their various narratives without apology. This can be significant as black masculinities still fall victim to the white gaze. Embraced as a strategy of white supremacy the white gaze emerges in various and different forms whose goal it is to maintain supremacy over sacred black masculinities. There are particular spaces established by white supremacy and agreed upon by black masculinities that denote a space where sacred black masculinities can exist and be controlled. This must be viewed as a problem to be eradicated beyond notions of economy and privilege. What I mean here is that the sacred black masculine must develop a transformational narrative.

They must move beyond but not forget the narrative of the middle passage and the plantation; becoming those new horizons of love and life or, as Martin Luther King Jr. would say, *A Testament of Hope*.[30] A call goes out to re-imagine sacred black masculinities, to liberate them from the vestiges of white supremacy. Reflecting on the words of Patricia Hill Collins[31], a black feminist and scholar, there must be a reconceptualization of race, class and gender from

28 Nkrumah. Consciencism. Philosophy and Ideology for Decolonization and Development with particular reference to the Africa Revolution, 78.

29. Hooks. We Real Cool, Black Men and Masculinity, 23.

30. King, Jr. A *Testament of Hope, the essential writings and speeches of Martin Luther King Jr.*

31. Collins. *Black Feminist Thought: Knowledge, Consciousness, and the Politics of Empowerment,* 221–238.

constructs of interlocking oppressions to constructs of authenticity and as such liberation. Black feminist thought, addressed here as a means to decolonize the mind of the sacred black masculine, provides a structure or a framework which could, if employed, create a liberative framework for mental and social transformation.

The situation of the black man must be considered a compelling narrative calling him to invest in new sociocultural and theological ground. This ground, consisting of a deep, rich soil composed of memories embodied in sacred black masculinities, must reflect those cultural, historical and diaspora experiences of the black man, creating a distinct space of sacred blackness without apology. What I mean is that sacred black masculinities must be that creative space of intent as it peels back the layers of identity shaped by historical interlocking oppressions. Of course one might ask, "What is authentic blackness?" This question becomes one more reason to peel back those layers of historical interlocking oppressions, to interrogate what it really means to be black.

In contrast, yet at the same time similar in its reception by normative sensibilities, the divine black transgender feminine is considered to be evil by some, an assault on pseudo-sacred norms. She becomes an opportunity for ridicule; she is the other, considered a particular abomination perpetrated on society, a performance of male privilege perpetrated on an insecure, narcissistic culture and society. An agent of the indecent, she transcends the boundaries of gender queering notions of ontological legitimacy in the face of church and society. She presents the profane of God, of the cross, even of the untouchable. She presents God's invitation for all to experience the genuine love of God as she moves in the spirit of the living God.

The divine black transgender feminine presents a sacred bodily space of significant difference within the context of a hetero-normative mindset. This difference, flowing and immersing and even queering those arbitrary boundaries, paint a distinct picture of the permeability of identity. That said, this discourse on sacred black masculinities and the divine black transgender feminine provides a space to access the prophetic hope embodied in a real sacred presence.

I am told that the reality in regard to gender and sexual identity has changed. I have yet to actually experience this truth outside of progressive academic communities and certain progressive media like MSNBC or NPR. Seemingly, the world outside of progressive academic/media discourse is, for the most part, still reflecting notions dictated by norms established for and by the production of white supremacy.

NOTIONS ON CULTURAL STUDIES AND CRITICAL THEORY

A discourse on gender, sexuality and race emerge as a post-colonial and post-modern question of agency. Who owns the testicles and the vagina, and to whom do they owe their allegiance? Who owns the name, description and body parts of the person? I remember when I first went to change my name I was astonished that neither my name nor my identity were my own. In fact there was a cost for changing *my* name, which I, a struggling black transgender woman could not afford, and this cost was paid to the state of California. Clearly the state's interest in my name change, even my body, was a matter of control, hence the cost. Yet beyond its desire to control identity I ask "What does a name represent to the society and/or culture, particularly to a structure of racial hetero-patriarchy still in the throes of a global war on terrorism maintained through no-fly lists, drones and an ever emerging police state?"

Homi Bhaba, in his book *The Location of Culture*, 1994 writes, post-colonial criticism bears witness to the unequal and uneven forces of cultural representation involved in the contest for political and social authority within the modern world order."[32] Considering Homi Bhaba's apt description/definition of post-colonial criticism, the act of naming and the integrity of the process become a means to maintain a particular regime. I propose to use

32. Bhaba. *The Location of Culture*, 245.

it here as a tool towards the liberation of gender and sexuality. I find it to be a critical tool for the liberation of gender and sexuality from their heteronormative characterization as a fixed colonized space. As such, a different notion of culture historical studies, using post-colonial criticism within a cultural historical analysis becomes a means of decentering and decanonizing normative notions of gender and sexuality.

Cultural historical studies are frameworks for developing a different notion of culture and history but also a means of interrogating the legitimacy of the heteronormative complex. Cultural historical studies can provide critical apprehension towards a new paradigm of liberation. Ben Agger, Professor of Sociology at the State University of New York at Buffalo, in his book *Cultural Studies and Critical Theory* writes,

> "One of the central insights of cultural studies is that there is no single or singular version of it. In a certain sense, a cultural study resists programmatism—a definitive as a methodology and a discrete list of critical topics. Culture is found in every corner of late-capitalist society, undercutting the high-culture/popular-culture distinction. Thus, cultural studies resist canonization of cultural products on which it focuses its attention. There is no canon, only heterogeneity of culture gestures, from science to science fiction."[33]

Based on the words of Agger, cultural studies is an intersectional ground for the deconstruction of those structures and frameworks of domination which inhibit the authentic voice as well as authentic critique. Cultural studies as a methodology must have as its primary directive the mining of the authentic voice. I must acknowledge both implicitly and explicitly that a normative culture is non-existent. Rather, as Agger states, culture in the broad anthropological sense is any expressive activity contributing to social learning.[34]

33. Agger. *Cultural Studies as Critical Theory*, 2–3.
34. Ibid.

He further writes, "the expansion of the notion of culture by students of cultural studies, of which I am one, affects the ways in which popular culture is now conceptualized as a broad ensemble of everyday discursive practices that may well fall outside the traditional parameters of official culture narrowly defined, and the ways that science is conceptualized as cultural discourse itself."[35] As an individual who identifies as divine transfemme and sacred masculine I find that culture, based on Aggers concept of culture, consists of various practices of faith, including its rituals, strategies of pedagogy, movements and language to be a defining framework of transgender culture. "Cultural studies both renders science self-reflexively discursive in post-positivist fashion and at the same time engages in a kind of meta-canonization (or, better, a deconstruction of canon) that opens cultural analysis to all sorts of interpretive possibilities, all the way from conversation analysis."[36]

I think it prudent and even necessary to have a discussion on post-structuralist, post-modernism and the crisis of identity and representation particularly as this thesis grapples with orientations towards transformation. "Post-structuralism refers to the theory of knowledge and language associated with the work of Jacques Derrida (1976, 1978, 1981, and 1987)."[37]

This perspective suggests that language users do not just pluck words out of thin air or a thesaurus when trying to convey meaning, fitting them to the objects or feelings being conveyed.[38] Instead, the meanings of words largely determine what we end up saying. In effect, post-structuralism reconstructs the process of meaning in a way that gives fuller weight to the pre-given meanings imbedded not only in particular words but in relation of words (Saussure's signs) to each other.[39] As a result, Derrida argues that meaning is forever elusive and incomplete in the sense that

35. Agger. *Cultural Studies as Critical Theory,* 2–3.
36. Ibid.
37. Ibid, 93.
38. Ibid.
39. Ibid.

language can never perfectly convey what is meant by the language use.[40]

Post-modernism for its part is a theory of cultural, intellectual and societal discontinuity that rejects the linearism of enlightenment notions of progress.[41] History is no longer conceived as going somewhere, from pre-history to the end of history. The present is no longer experienced as a way station en route to something higher or better. Nor is the past to be reconstructed as a dim period of mythic and prejudice. Instead, post-modern culture draws on the best in a variety of historical epochs, indulging in a studied eclecticism.[42]

Post-structuralism and post-modernism theory should be contextualized for the demands of American intellectual and social life. The translation of post-structuralist theorists with our rhetorical resonances, linguistics, and discursive habits challenges national biases and intellectual insularities on both sides of the Atlantic. I must grit the smooth surface of post-structuralist theories—which often enjoy untroubled travel to our intellectual shores—with specificities of our gender identity and ethnicity.[43]

Based on what I consider to be the hope embedded in post-structuralism and post-modernism the question now emerges, "How can the divine transgender-feminine and the sacred masculine, engaged here as strategies of liberation, participate in the deconstruction of imperial notions gender identity?" These strategies are necessarily critical and prophetic, critiquing cultural, social, political and religious sensibilities. To some extent this work is a response to my dear departed sister Marcella Althaus-Reid who challenged notions of gender and sexuality in her book *Indecent Theology, Theological Perversions in Sex, Gender and Politics*.[44]

40. Agger. *Cultural Studies as Critical Theory,* 93.

41. Ibid.

42. Ibid.

43. Ibid.

44. Althaus-Reid. *Indecent Theology, Theological Perversions in Sex, Gender and Politics.*

That said, I suggest that this work is an attempt to respond to the poignant cry of mysister. Using the works of Bell Hooks, Audre Lorde, Joseph Beam, James Baldwin, Franz Fanon, Patricia Hill Collins, Emanuel Levinas, Cornel West, Michael Eric Dyson and others, this work will seek to engage this very real crisis and the opportunity and hope embedded within.

Chapter 2

Embodied Memories and Teachings of My Neighborhood

M emory is the soil that produces a harvest of emotion and movement in the individual and the community, revealing various intergenerational visions, images and hopes. Memories, plumb the depths of the soul, presenting questions that challenge as well as affirm identity. As such, memory has moral and ethical bearing within the lived experience and the various contexts of social themes, social inquiry and social change.

Memories can teach us how to respond to the personal, the multi-layered and multi-faceted society and its various dynamic challenges. Memory is vast, affecting every facet and moment of everyday life. They are foundational to the acquisition of consciousness. As such, the question that emerges ––at least for this writer –– is, "How do we live in the presence of memory?" Memory casts a long shadow over the present. Memories of people, places, relationships, loneliness, failings, desires for undiscovered country and prophetic moments and movements of *Coming Out* are significant crystallizing lessons of life necessarily creating a space for imagination and re-imagination.

As I write and re-write these words, engaging memories of my life, I encounter memories as a means to reflect on past experiences, seeking to give voice to those *formative touchstones*[1] that reveal life, for me, as a liberative work of art. Life, received as a liberative work of art of divine cosmic origin engages the depth of a soul yearning to be, invoking fantastic even uncanny movements of joy, loss, fruitfulness, pain, suffering and impermanence which become the brushes of a divine, even a mystical imagination. It shapes identity, giving it character, definition and meaning with implications towards public and social life in culture and society. Identity is a sacred embodiment of memory. Memories are full of implications toward the political and social transformation of societies. Memory is a queer framework that holds the confluences of human and divine action suggesting that life is a prophetic action of divine import.

> *Life is a journey of memory, gathering points of self-discovery. Memory thus emerges as an impending mode of mystical divine presence. Life is an impassioned plea of a cosmic universal joy.*

Born and raised in South Central Los Angeles in the 1960's, my sister and I grew up in a family where my father worked as an aircraft engineer for a multi-national corporation and my mother worked as a teacher's aide at my local elementary school and a social worker for the County of Los Angeles. Dad was a strong man of faith and a member of the local African Methodist Episcopal Church. He worked hard to take care of our family. My mother was a strong woman of faith who I would see reading her Bible every morning before she started her day. Looking back on that time I find that her reading the Bible every morning had an influence on my calling into ministry.

My youth was full of diversity where people of diverse backgrounds and identities were embraced. I remember a man who wore a straw hat riding a horse in the middle of our street; I remember thinking, Wow that's cool. I remember there was a really big oak tree across from our house where men and women would

---

1. Tanaka. Formative Touchstones, Finding Place as a Teacher Through and Indigenous Learning Experience in Memory and Pedagogy, 60.

gather to talk about the day's events, i.e., business, sports and matters of neighborhood importance. I'm sure that tree has a lot of stories to tell. Gatherings of celebration, sorrows, hopes and blessings of empowerment codified a people rooted in an uncommon faith.

This was a time of political and social upheavals, when my neighborhood friends and family were clear that the Los Angeles City Police Department and City officials did not have our best interest at heart. It was also a time when the depth of the oppression was evidenced by the drunkenness and the violence of men and women who sought drink and/or fight to somehow sooth their sorrows and miseries. Burning fishtail Cadillacs, Watts riots, the Watts Towers, members of the Black Panther Party and the civil rights movement characterized my childhood experiences, both women and men participating in protests against racial and social injustice.

I remember, as a kid, those times in my neighborhood were times of imagination and curiosity. I would look at the people, their actions and the events that shaped and characterized my neighborhood. I am reminded of people who today would be called transgender who lived in my South Central Los Angeles neighborhood. Reflecting on that time I remember they lived in a small cream-colored house on the corner across from the liquor store. From time to time I would see both men and women and sometimes the police enter their front door and come out some hours later.

As I would watch them from afar, through my upstairs bedroom window on the second floor of my childhood home, my curiosity was piqued. Something inside of me resonated with what I saw as they lived the life, which I perceived was the fullness of their authentic selves. Walking the streets, going shopping at the local grocery store, talking with neighbors, just living their life without inhibition was, for a young teenage boy a love supreme, to use the words of John Coltrane.

Through my neighborhood I was taught that race, like gender identity and sexuality, is a primary evidential construct grounded in empire and governed by religious, political and economic interests. That said, there was a consistent, even persistent violation of the body by an empire, represented by the Los Angeles Police Department, that experienced the black body as criminal and a threat. Memories of my neighborhood of youth bring forth a cognizance that I embody the teachings and intimacies of my neighborhood in South Central Los Angeles. Its life, its truth and its presence flow through me. I am impressed that my neighborhood has provided me form and content to develop a unique voice to advocate for the concerns and issues in the human community. As I reflect on the neighborhood of my youth I am confronted with a life that was cradled in the bosom of my neighborhood.

I realize that the strength to come out as an activist for the liberation of gender from the oppressive structures was instilled by the neighborhood of my youth. In my memory the neighborhood of my youth appears as that sacred place of radical baptism. At this point I must offer a space of clarity. Baptism was not an initiation into the Kindom of God but into a world of Howard Thurman's Jesus and the disinherited.[2]

It was a baptism into the struggle of the African in America. This struggle has been a burden on the soul and spirit of the African in Diaspora yet this burden has also been the touchstone from which the Diasporic African has lived a type of liberation from the historical oppression. It is a liberation based in mystical empowerment, rooted, grounded and formed out of the faith of the African mothers and fathers. It is a faith that kept many in the middle passage knowing that their God was intimately engaged in their struggles. Achieving liberation, then, for the daughters and sons of the middle passage could not be attained without the faith presented here as the black church. The black church, due to rampant oppressions, has been that stubborn center as well as the challenge for the African American community in its struggle for gender and sexuality liberation. Yet even with its challenges, the black church has been a key component in the formation of African-American identity.

2. Thurman. *Jesus and the disinherited.*

That said, the neighborhood of my youth is a "prophetic fragment."[3] It is that critical illumination of the crisis in American religion and culture. In my memory it becomes that cry for those living in their silent agonies. As my memory releases gushers of living water I must write haltingly , seeking to contribute to a discursive space within black criticism to address issues pertaining to a reconceptualization of gender and discourse in the black community. My journey of gender then emerges as a divine strategy towards a different conception of humanity grounded in the historical black faith of African mothers and fathers. It is also grounded in a progressive black community, an intimate encounter with gender and an ever-increasing knowledge of the human experience.

A reconceptualization of gender is an articulation of the criticalities and visions that emerge out of memory. As I remember the struggles to live as deemed by society, those struggles become the ground of inspiration for the liberation of gender from Franz Fanon's white gaze. Memory is an avenue toward the liberation of critical difference from the pathological need for agreement and sameness. Of course, for some people, the divine transgender feminine and the sacred black masculine may be considered a radical strategy toward a Black Pantheresque resistance movement.

Yet the plight of gender must be addressed in order for gender to emerge from the closet imposed by notions and interpretations of binarism. It is hoped that this study will be received as an invitation for a broader, more liberative discourse on gender and its implications toward critical difference. As I write this paper, I recount Renee T. White's words, "*Revolutionary struggle and resistance always involve multileveled transformation.*"[4] Her words remind me that the reconceptualization and the re-imagining of gender will transform not only the black community but also American culture and society as whole. To assist in the reconceptualiza-

3. West. *Prophetic Fragments Illumination of the Crisis in American Religion & Culture.*

4. White. Revolutionary Theory: Sociological Dimensions of Fanon Sociological Dimensions of Fanon's Sociologie d'une revolution revolutionary

tion of gender this paper will engage the action event of coming out. Coming Out in the context of this paper is a coming out of a mindset immersed in systems and processes of binary thinking.

Chapter 3

Oh God, I'm Coming Out

Queer thoughts on Coming Out
and Representation from the Perspective
of the Divine Black Transgender Feminine
and the Sacred Black Masculine

*C*oming Out is rarely a peaceful affair. It happens within a complex web of family, friends, colleagues, and communities of faith. It is emotionally, physically, religiously and spiritually charged. It can open a vortex of conflict with longstanding narrow mindsets and ways of being necessarily causing serious and, at times, violent tensions. That said, "Coming out" is not for the faint of heart, yet ultimately it is a blessing for all presenting God's coming out party.

Now I must confess that, contrary to normative philosophies of a hegemonic individualism, "Coming Out" is not always a matter of choice but is more of an evolution, or more appropriately an organic emergence of ontological import. I suppose if it were a choice, the only choice would be to live a life of denial, which has significant mental and spiritual health implications. More so, Coming Out represents an evolution of the human being rooted sustainability, in cosmological consciousness and intellectual intent beyond mindsets oriented towards human constructs of colonization.

Hence my experience of *"Coming Out"* as a black intellectual who presents both the transgender feminine and the sacred masculine in a culture and society where binary frameworks of racial superiority/inferiority, hegemonic masculinity, evidenced by common dualities such as white-black, good-evil, male-female, heterosexual-homosexual and mind-matter; the characteristics that American culture lifts up in various forms and media as the normative[1] has been challenging on many levels.

My experience as an intellectual and activist for the liberation of gender has made me cognizant of the lack of black transgender intellectuals in this pursuit. Academic conferences such as the American Academy of Religion (AAR) or the Transgender Religious Leaders Summit (TRLS), or the Human Rights Campaign (HRC) have been a rigorous and lonely endeavors. Seemingly, once I left the religious scene I left the community of the black transgender women.

I find myself in a sort of dilemma. My choice to be an intellectual has caused me to be marginalized within the black transgender community. I face what Cornel West terms a grim predicament. In the chapter entitled, Dilemma of the Black Intellectual in his book *Keeping the Faith, Philosophy of Race in America*, he writes, "caught between an insolent American society and an insouciant black community, the African-American who takes seriously the life of the mind inhabits an isolated and insulated world. This condition has little to do with the motives and intentions of black intellectuals; rather it is an objective situation created by circumstances not of their own choosing."[2]

My choice to come out as a black transgender intellectual emerged as I came in close contact with a small group of black scholars in the transgender community, becoming good friends and allies in the liberation of gender. These scholars were not

---

1. Mutua. *Theorizing Progressive Black Masculinities* in Progressive Masculinities, ed. Anthena D. Mutua, 12.

2. West. *Keeping the Faith Philosophy and Race in America*, 67.

bourgeois but were organic intellectuals being grounded in their particular transgender experience and the need to understand the profoundness of who they were within the context of everyday life. Now I want to suggest here that transgender scholarship, particularly black transgender scholarship, is still on the periphery of the academy, and still in development, residing on the margins. My experience suggests that the infrastructure for the transgender scholar is still in its early stages of gaining respect and support in both the white and black intelligencia.

I am fortunate to be a member of a community of faith that seeks to combine the scholar-intellectualwith the activism based on an understanding of the historical connection between the two. There is a recognition that while prayer, sacred text, the preached word and support groups are a significant help on the journey to wholeness, the deep historical oppressions of race, gender and sexuality require holistic strategies to break the bondage and to give the member access to their liberation provided through the life, work and ministry of Jesus of Nazareth. In this context the role of the scholar-intellectual is to be engaged in artful healing.

Artful healing, at least from the standpoint of the scholar-intellectual, requires significant deconstruction of oppressive systems and structures. In her book *Enfleshing Freedom,* M. Shawn Copeland, Associate Professor of Theology at Boston College writes, "Given the location and conditions of [black] bodies in empire, the virulent global persistence of racism, xenophobia, re-actions to "illegal" or undocumented anti-bodies within the body of empire, the bodies maimed and slaughtered in wars mounted by clients of empire, the bodies done to death by AIDS and hunger and abuse, and above all that body broken and resurrected for us, theological anthropology can never cease speaking of bodies."[3] For me the words of Copeland go directly to the importance of the scholar-intellectual in the struggle for the liberated mind and body.

The scholar-intellectual is an active agent in the artful healing of the body. The concept of artful healing emerges out of the need

3. Copeland. *Enfleshing Freedom, body, race and being,* 57.

for the person to invest in a different imagination of themselves and the world around them. As a person who continually seeks to embrace all of who I am, regardless of gain or loss, I have lived out a different imagination of my humanity. For me living out a different imagination of humanity has meant embracing all of who I am beyond cultural and societal norms. Living out a different imagination I experience a certain depth of liberation of the mind, heart, soul and body. This has been a long and difficult journey, yet the question at the heart of who I am as an intellectual and a person of faith is a question of authenticity. Living a different imagination then in the final analysis is living authentically in spite of and regardless of the normative cultural or societal discourse.

Living authentically as a black transgender woman, encountering looks of hatred and disgust on the faces of people, as well as being verbally accosted on a San Francisco street, I have become particularly aware of the multiple forms of violence that oppression can produce in the individual. Particularly in the black community, the depth of the oppression is experienced verbally, physically and spiritually, a violation of what I term here as critical difference. The black community then becomes the rampant, and albeit irrational defense, even pursuit of the very oppression that seemingly inhibits the black imagination. This oppression sets boundaries on where and how critical difference is lived out. I find that the only place the African-America transgender woman can get any respect at all (and even this is under discussion) is seemingly on the drag scene. I remember questioning a colleague at church about using "drag" in the Transgender Day of Remembrance. I was looking for something more reflective, more intellectually provocative.

In contrast to my experience as a black transgender woman the dynamic, divine experiences of some of my white transgender sisters show that they are much more diverse in living out their transgender experience. Not only are they significant in the drag community, doing great work in the areas of charity, they are also in the corporate world. They are professors, scholars, CEOs, even mainstream entertainers. They write books, have television shows, they run the gamut. More than any other group they are the most successful overall within the transgender community. My impression is that the greatest benefit the white transgender woman enjoys is that they still function out of their white male power base. In contrast the black transgender women's community doesn't have that same power base. As such, within the transgender community stratifications of race, economics, and education become significant hyper detractors. Let me be clear, the circle of successful white transgender women I encounter, while significant within the transgender community, is small within the overall American human narrative, and are warriors in the continuing gender warfare.

REEMERGENCE OF THE BLACK MALE AS QUEER IN CONTRAST WITH THE BLACK TRANSGENDER WOMAN AND THE QUEST FOR A NEW LOCUS OF LEGITIMACY

My re-emergence as a black man occurred as a consequence of a very real intimate relationship where the need arose to acknowledge the expansiveness of my gender narrative, which evolved through the black male gender identity and continued through the transgender feminine. After the initial shock, my partner, who had met me when I lived as a transgender woman, began to embrace the male identity even more than they embraced transgender woman identity. As the relationship began to grow and deepen, the male identity took center stage, displacing the transgender feminine as the primary gender identity, necessarily opening a tense and contested gendered space under the rubric gender identity integration.

The goal was to introduce them to all of who I was. Looking back on the relationship, my impression is that at the point of revelation the transgender woman who I had lived out as a matter of authenticity for fourteen years was now a sidebar conversation. I chose to use the term queer as part of the re-emergence to acknowledge the expansiveness of my gendered experience. Consequently, I was unable to fit all of who I was within the relationship.

The relationship slowly devolved into a relationship based in colonized, i.e. traditional notions of relationships established by the slave master or plantation owner. All of the socialization processes in which I was formed came into clear view and clarity. Now as a black transgender woman, living in community and alone, I had the freedom, even liberty, to live as I pleased. Now living in a relationship based solely on traditional values came into play. Discussion of racism, economics and politics ruled the day but discussions on gender and its fluidity were filled with tension or just not allowed. It was as if the person who I had met in a discussion of gender now dismissed the conversation outright.

The relationship became untenable. Over time it became an oppressive living situation which I had to leave. It was costly. I only reveal this situation to give flesh to the power of colonization and oppression in the black community. While the black male, socialized as a colonized border identity was accepted, even celebrated and embraced, the transgender woman I was and am now was relegated as a sidebar conversation seldom discussed. My life within this relationship was a complex discourse of integrative negotiations and notions of critical difference.

Conflicting and contrasting realities, immersed in silence, emerged causing significant tensions. It was a difficult and complicated task with implications towards the articulated and interrelated realms of race, gender and class. In this process I found that my experience of gender was, at least in my estimation post-colonial, in that I experienced it as a critique of colonized notions of gender. As such, I found that my experience of gender came in direct conflict with the imperial socialization processes critiqued, yet at the same time tacitly accepted.

This experience made me even more cognizant of the interconnectedness of race, sexuality, gender and class within a white supremacy frame of production. The aforementioned then becomes one more motivation for this project. To envision the liberation of vision and representation and human relationships, whether intimate or institutional, from the narrow confines of identity production based on the premises established by racial and heteropatriarchy. The task was to merge the transgender woman and the queer male, to somehow blend the two very distinct vessel-identities. Now the male, in my view, is that part of me that I consider a colonized identity. He was familiar with a common socialization narrative. As such he was at liberty to move in the world since, to a certain extent, he represents the face of colonization. He is a man; subtlety in your face for the sake of his heart. He was that traditional body, the man who sacrifices/compromises himself for the sake of the family.

When identifying as a male I didn't struggle with the world because on the surface I represented the desires of the American society. I stayed within the boundaries of the sociocultural construction established in concert with and approved by the dominant narrative. I had a job, no problem with employment beyond the norm. In contrast my life as a queer black transgender woman represents a type of an anti-colonial or post-colonial narrative with different communities of accountability and liberties. My life now presents a radical, even critical difference; particular notions of polarization of cultural and societal notions of decency. I am authentic, divine and beautiful. I am who I am.

"Coming Out" must be considered care of the soul, a quest for that authentic space of personal divinity. Coming out is about *detaching* who I am and what I am about from the antiquated ideals of gender, grounded in the Atlantic slave trade and the master-slave narrative of the plantation, desires of white supremacy.[4] Cornel West writes in *Black Strivings in twilight of Civilization,* "White Supremacy dictates the boundaries of American Democracy -- with black folk the indispensable sacrificial lamb vital to its sustenance. Hence, black subordination constitutes the necessary condition for the flourishing of American democracy, the tragic prerequisite for America itself. This is, in part, what Richard Wright meant when he noted, "The Negro is America's metaphor."[5] That said, challenging these ideals uncovers significant and dynamic

---

4. Copeland. Enfleshing Freedom, body, race and being, 110–116.

5. West. Black Strivings in a twilight of Civilization, The Cornel West Reader, 98.

gender(s) that represent a particular divergence from "traditional" American culture so eloquently noted by Professor West.

In her provocative book, *Progressive Black Masculinities*, Anthena D. Mutua writes, "Though this ideal is dominant or hegemonic, it is not the only idea of masculinity. In fact, through the lived experiences of people and their interactions with their societies, multiple ideas and practices emerge to constitute masculinity differently over time and space."[6] An exploration of black masculinities calls into question the current framework of masculinity to a point where the ideal set forth by the elite white heterosexual male is radically deconstructed.

Developing a different concept of gender is a challenging task; to create a space, or a framework for the liberation of gender *from* a discourse grounded in the imagination of white supremacy is indeed a generational calling yet worthy of the liberation of the human soul. This must be considered significant as it questions the origin of the black identity in the American context, which I suspect becomes the source of various forms of hatred and self-hatred. It identifies one persistent question presented by June Jordan, a poet and activist in her book *Civil Wars Observations from the Front Lines of America*, "Body and Soul, Black America reveals the extreme questions of contemporary life, questions of freedom and identity: How can I be who I am?"[7] For me, as a black transgender woman who identifies as a queer in the 21st century, the implications of Jordan's question are nothing less than a radical break from traditional understandings of ontological presence. Her question implies a yearning and a longing to explore a different imagination of gender identity beyond identities imposed.

A thesis which addresses a reconceptualization of gender is particularly relevant in a time when the African-American male is experiencing increased incarceration rates, continued disenfranchisement, high unemployment rates, low standards of education, and a mortality rate higher than the national average in the midst

---

6. Mutua. *Theorizing Progressive Black Masculinities* in Progressive Masculinities, 13.

7. Jordan. *Civil Wars Observations from the Front Lines of America*, 46.

of an American president who identifies as a black man. In her excellent book, *The New Jim Crow* Michelle Alexander writes, "More African-American adults are under correctional control today -- in prison or jail, on probation or parole -- than were enslaved in 1850, a decade before the Civil War began.

The mass incarceration of people of color is a big part of the reason that a black child born today is less likely to be raised by both parents than a black child born during slavery."[8] Alexander presents the crisis of the African-American male and his family as a victim of systematic marginalization curiously imposed by white supremacist structures. She further writes, "The clock has been turned back on racial progress in America, though scarcely anyone seems to notice."[9] I was a part of a ministers group that ministered in a small, gated African-American community in Richmond, California where drugs, unemployment and single parent households were the norm. This particular neighborhood, while not representative of all African-American neighborhoods, uncovered the very real impact of the New Jim Crow. Some African-American neighborhoods are in a precarious state. They have become altogether places of peril and hopelessness reflecting a peculiar reality of loss and grief. Notions of community and love have been displaced by a lack of trust and compromised ethics.

From the perspective of the cultural-historical theorist the following questions emerge, "How is white desire reflected in those communities?" Do gender, sexuality, economics and even religion reflect, to some extent, white desire? Is the need for the African-American to be "respectable" in the face of Franz Fanon's white gaze more prescient than the criticality of black masculinities or for that matter the divine black transgender feminine? I suggest here that the work of Franz Fanon is critical if the transgender feminine and the sacred black masculinities are to be actualized as legitimate and equitable modes of identity. The Fanonian Project of "Decolonizing Psychiatry," where European trained psychiatrists, up to

8. Alexander. *The New Jim Cross Mass Incarceration in the Age of Colorblindness,* 175.

9 Ibid.

Fanon's time, were agents of French colonization. In this project Fanon asks salient questions about psychiatry and its impact on the liberation of the colonial mind. What kind of psychiatry is possible in the post-colony? What should be its goals? To discipline and control? To facilitate reintegration into society? What is the role of the psychiatrist? These are important questions even today as white supremacy and the white imagination still inhabit the collective American psyche. Fanon's questions of cultural context provide a significant basis for the mental and emotional strength to create a sacred space of diversity. In his book, *Black Skin, White Masks* Franz Fanon writes,

> "I arrive slowly in the world; sudden emergences are no longer my habit. I crawl along. The white gaze, the only valid one, is already dissecting me. I am fixed. Once their microtomes are sharpened, the Whites objectively cut sections of my reality. I have been betrayed. I sense, I see in this white gaze that it's the arrival not of a new man, but of a new type of man, a new species. A Negro in fact!"[10]

I suggest that Fanon's reflection aptly describes my own reflective experience as I grapple with the reality of the white gaze as I ministered in this particular African-American community. The impact of the white gaze on the African-American community has had a particularly negative effect in matters of gender, sexuality, economic, health and wholeness considerations. To use Fanon's words, "[T]he white world, the only decent one, was preventing me from participating"[11] in my own criticality. In light of the aforementioned, the reconceptualization of black masculinities becomes significant within African-American discourse and the development of African-American culture beyond the white gaze.

In a discourse on cultural-historical studies the theorist interrogates social-political religious and economic movements as that critical witness that critiques structures of access and identity. Therefore, the cultural-historical theorist, as an intellectual on the

10. Franz Fanon. *Black Skin, White Masks*, 95.

11. Ibid.

left, seeks to link the philosophical and the real human dynamics of culture and society. Bell Hooks quotes in her book *Outlaw Culture, Resisting Representation* in the chapter *Seeing and Making Culture Representing the Poor* (1994) the following words of Cornel West,

> ". . . black intellectuals within the "professional–manage-rial class in U.S. advance capitalist society" must engage in a kind of critical self-inventory, a historical situating and positioning of ourselves as persons who reflect on the situation of those more disadvantaged than us even though we may have relatives and friends in the black underclass."[12]

For me Cornel West's words suggest that the cultural-histor-ical theorist, as a part of the academic "professional-managerial class,"[13] should do a critical self-inventory as they position them-selves in the situation and/or circumstance of the disadvantaged. Advocacy then for West must be more than an academic pursuit; it must be an extension of communal intimacy. The actions of Cor-nel West gift him as that intimate critical witness that embodies that prophetic tradition so desperately needed in our communities today.

I met Cornel West at the American Academy of Religion conference in San Francisco, California. We had a short but rich and intimate conversation about his involvement in the economic and social liberation movements and what they mean to various factions. This brother is *deep,* went through my mind, as I listened to him, a leading black public Intellectual. Here was a man who celebrated life; its dynamic intimacy and philosophical thought, weaving them together to make a new culture with a different imagination of identity.

I found Cornel West to be in a similar vein to James Baldwin, a writer and activist of the mid-twentieth century who lived in the South of France due to the rampant racial and sexual violence

---

12. Hooks. *Seeing and Making Culture, Representing the Poor in Outlaw Culture Resisting Representations,* 165.

13. Franz Fanon. *Black Skin, White Masks,* 166.

against homosexuals in United States.[14] Born and raised in Harlem, Baldwin was a black gay man of deep critical thought and substance. He was a man who approached life with an intimate uncompromising allegiance to socio-cultural and political justice. Through his provocative writing Baldwin exposed the lies imposed on society by "white fantasies of desire"[15] manifested through various forms of media and economic models secured through state, i.e. white terrorism. "He knew all too well the pitfalls of being at the margins of many identities that were thought to be exclusive (gay and black and American, for example)."[16] He grappled with the competing discourses of race, gender, sexuality and poverty exposing elegantly and sometimes inelegantly the dynamic complexity of the human being.

"Baldwin is [compelling] and large; containing multitudes! And Baldwin has spoken to most every issue of great importance in our time."[17] Dwight McBride's summation of Baldwin resonates with me as I too grapple with these issues today. In his book *The Fire Next Time* James Baldwin writes, "[t]o be sensual. . . is to respect and rejoice in the force of life, of life itself, and to be present in all that one does, from the effort of love to the breaking of bread."[18] The theorist then must share in the joys, burdens, sorrows and challenges of the community; this being a matter of cultural integrity and, I would add, a compelling need to love.

Baldwin's words are reminiscent of my youth growing up in the local African Methodist Episcopal (AME) Church where we would sing "Let us Break Bread together on our knees, Let us break bread together on our knees," When I fall on My knees with My

---

14. Wallace. *"I'm Not Entirely What I Look Like"* in James Baldwin Now ed. Dwight A. McBride, 296.

15. Ross. *White Fantasies of Desire, Baldwin and the Racial Identities* in James Baldwin Now ed. Dwight A. McBride, 13.

16. McBride. *"How Much Time Do You Want for Your Progress?"* New Approaches to Baldwin, 2.

17. Ibid.

18. Baldwin. *The Fire Next Time*, pp. 43.

Face to the Rising Sun, Oh Lord Have Mercy on Me"[19] every first Sunday during the breaking of bread. It is this breaking of bread that is at the center of black cultural-historical experience. For the African-American cultural-historical theorist then "breaking bread" becomes an act of making culture.[20]

Years later when I came out as a transgender woman I joined the Metropolitan Community Church (MCC). It was a community of faith where people who identified as lesbian, gay, bisexual, transgender (LGBT), queer and allies broke bread together every Sunday. For me this was reminiscent of the first Sunday of my youth when my family would take communion at the local AME Church. For those who were involved in the struggles for civil rights, breaking bread was an acknowledgement of the social cost heaped on those who were different, yet it was also a sacred act that created a space for a voracious and progressive moral vision.

In the MCC Church breaking bread was significant for a marginalized population portrayed by certain conservative media, religious institutions and communities of faith as mentally ill, whorish, perverted, evil, lazy, shiftless and unworthy. In particular I remember being a student at Regent University in Virginia Beach, VA. It is a conservative University, founded by Pat Robertson in the late 1970's. While attending I started having transgender concerns and was directed to the psychology department. When I went to the psychologist she informed me that they did not have any issue with transgender people, but informed me that they treated transgender concerns as a mental health issue.

The local MCC was an act of invitation for a different imagination to emerge. It was an act that nurtured a unique voice to speak for a suffering humanity on the margins of society. Breaking bread revealed to me a calling to reconceptualize race, gender and sexuality—not only in terms of my faith but also as a necessary political action. My experience of Communion, Eucharist, or The

19. Hooks and Cornel West. *Breaking Bread, Insurgent Black Intellectual Life,* 1–2.

20. Hooks. *Seeing and Making Culture in* Outlaw Culture Resisting Representations, 165.

Lord's Supper at MCC, more than anything else, caused me to understand that who I am has historical significance.[21]

Considering that I am historically significant changes my awareness of myself, my actions and my communication. This is particularly important in building and reconceptualizing culture and society. Experiencing ourselves in terms of historical significance necessarily engenders an intimate encounter with *difference*. Difference in contrast to assimilation is sacred and powerful tending toward wholeness of individual and community. Difference in the context of this work represents the various differences in genders, sexualities, skin identifications and faith/religious persuasions. It is about the space between social, political and economic identification. As we move toward progressive conceptions of black masculinities embracing differences become key factors in developing strategies that empower those people who identify as male and black to overcome barriers to their criticality.

In her book *Sister Outsider,* Audre Lorde, a black lesbian poet and feminist, writes that racism, sexism, heterosexism and homophobia are forms of human blindness.[22] She further writes, "[t] hey stem from the same root—an inability to recognize the notion of *difference* as a dynamic human force, one which is enriching rather than threatening to the defined self, when there are shared goals."[23] I suggest that for Lorde *difference* is the locus of legitimacy and a sacred luminal space of a critical voice in pursuit of shared goals. It is when we speak from our place of difference and not assimilation that *our* voice emerges. *Difference is pregnant with meaning.* Therefore, intimacies must lean towards differences as we work towards the dismantling of barriers. The words of Lorde teach me the importance of our differences and how to hold and define our differences for ourselves and not let it be defined for us.

I embrace the words of Lorde who writes, "As a Black lesbian feminist, I have a particular feeling, knowledge, and understanding

21. Tinney. *Why a Black Church?* In the Life. A Black Gay Anthology ed. Joseph Beam, 57.

22. Audre Lorde. *Sister Outsider*, pp. 45.

23 Ibid., 45.

49

for those sisters and brothers with whom I danced hard, played or even fought; who seek to embrace or even understand difference."[24] This deep participation has often been the forerunner for joint concerted actions not possible before. "[25] Since coming out years ago I have found that there are more queer/transgender people embracing difference. This embrace of difference has resulted in various political actions.

While the words of Lorde speak specifically to black women and their struggles, I suggest that her profound insights might be applied to other marginalized groups seeking to take hold and live in their difference. Embracing our difference in relation to defining ourselves for ourselves becomes increasingly important as we encounter societal and cultural authorities that are seemingly insensitive to realities beyond binary gender and sexuality discourses. Defining ourselves then has the very real potential of creating and developing a significant voice in the community with startling implications toward social justice and those policies that make for a more just and whole society.

What I am seeking here is a new consciousness not based in white supremacy, whiteways of being or the white gaze. The implications of this statement are nothing less than the emergence of a new discourse that enables and empowers access to *critical difference*. I suggest that critical difference, as used in the context of this thesis, goes beyond Audre Lorde's concept of *difference* to embrace prophetic identities which are beyond current notions of difference. In other words, *who we are* is no longer sifted through white visions with its academic underpinning, legislative laws, economics or corporate media, which tend to lead to self-hatred. In the context of this work, self-hatred is self-disgust: shame resulting from a strong dislike of yourself or your actions.

Self-hatred manifests as those of us who are critically different look in a mirror not made to reflect their particular critical difference. This mirror reflects the various religious, cultural, political and corporate media; representing dominant and primarily white

24. Audre Lorde, *Sister Outsider*, 59.
25 Ibid.

sensibilities. Self-hatred manifests as the full weight of American structures of domination fall upon those who are different. In light of the aforementioned I want to suggest that *critical difference* is an oppositional term that seeks to de-cloak the whiteness that undergirds current notions of difference which informs common discourse around issues of diversity. Critical difference then has the potential to become the new locus of legitimacy. Paul Robeson Jr., in his book *Black Ways of Seeing from "Liberty" to Freedom* writes,

> "I am a free Black American. I have a distinct culture. It derives from the traditional culture of African field slaves in the South. I identify with that culture by capitalizing the "B" in Black. Some people say, "Why make so much of a name? It's divisive in these times, when we need to bring everyone together." I reply, we can come together only if we say who we really are. We must stop pretending that in the United States of America being Black or being white is the same." Knowing who I am and what culture I come from is my foundation for leading a full and productive life. My roots in my own culture provide the doors and windows though which I communicate comfortably and constructively with others."[26]

I suggest that the words of Paul Robeson, Jr. reflect a consciousness shared by Audre Lorde and Cornel West, which advocates for a radical break from the long established locus of legitimacy towards a new locus of legitimacy based on critical difference. The implication of this break is nothing less than a dismantling of the American *Grand Narrative*.[27] According to Marcella Althaus-Reid (1952–2009), a Latin American theologian and author of Indecent Theology, "Grand narratives are authoritative discourses which sustain everyday life. They are ideologically constructed yet have assumed a natural and almost biological presence in our life."[28] This becomes the challenge to a new conception of critical differ-

---

26. Robeson, Jr., Black Way of Seeing from "Liberty" to Freedom, 1.

27. Reid. Indecent Theology, Theological Perversions in Sex, Gender and Politics, 11.

28. Ibid.

ence of which black masculinities and transgender femininity are part of new and different cultural component.

> *"Those of critical difference formerly the obscene now represent the liberation of destiny from the vestiges of whitenesss."*

The aforementioned statement on critical difference unleashes two thoughts (1) A strange freedom and (2) American destiny must no longer be linked to white supremacy or its desires. The first thought, *"A Strange Freedom"* rises from a Howard Thurman reader entitled *"A Strange Freedom, The Best of Howard Thurman on Religious Experience and Public Life."* The second thought, delinking American destiny from white supremacy rises from Homi Bhaba's book entitled *"The Location of Culture"* and the chapter entitled Interrogating Identity, Frantz Fanon and the postcolonial prerogative." I suggest here that both Thurman and Bhaba, though emerging from different contexts might have something to say about *those of critical difference* and the locus of legitimacy.

Thurman, the mystic, theologian and social activist awakens the soul to that intimate place of unity and interconnectedness, where divinity resides. Mysticism, then, for Thurman, being grounded in ethics, becomes that sacred place where the other encounters their unique and prophetic voice, within the wholeness of "all that is," here used as a metaphor for God or divine, and this a strange freedom indeed for one formerly in the shadows. For Thurman the goal of the mystic therefore is to know God in a comprehensive sense; for God is grasped in the whole as the whole self is laid hold upon God -- the vision of God is realized in inclusivity.[29] This becomes the ground of social change.

The implications of social change, i.e. cultural and societal tectonic shifts as experienced in the revolutions and social upheavals of the 20th and the beginnings of the 21st century, must be engaged through a process of "interrogation."[30] Interrogating iden-

---

29. Fluker and Tumber, eds. *A Strange Freedom, The Best of Howard Thurman on Religious Experience and Public life*, 108–109.

30. Homi Bhaba. *The Location of Culture*, 59.

tity, which I suggest here should be considered an intimate grace, emerges as an erotic longing for ultimate truth, which in the context of this work is post-colonial; even more so, it is anti-colonial, being a rejection of normative modes of being. It is subversive and an invitation to a "revolutionary awareness.[31]" Homi Bhaba, in his reading of Fanon writes of Fanon's vision, "What is the distinctive force of Fanon's vision? It comes, I believe, from the tradition of the oppressed, the language of a revolutionary awareness that, as Walter Benjamin suggests, 'the state of emergency in which we live is not the exception but the rule.'"[32]

"We must attain to a concept of history that is in keeping with this insight.' And the state of emergency is always a state of emergence."[33] Face it, those of us who cannot or refuse to adhere, or assimilate into whiteness and white supremacy and its various forms of totalitarianism, are consistently in a state of emergency. And this is the daily reality of the other, the unwanted, even the obscene, that they represent a transgression of white supremacy and exist in a state of emergency.

That said, an emergency has the very real potential to be that eschatological moment where the normative state of vision is challenged and expanded, introducing a new narrative into the temporal shape and space of time. Not long ago I was at a religious convocation in Las Vegas, NV. I had just finished a workshop and decided to get a bite to eat. Well, as I entered the space heads turned, mouths dropped open as if an explosion had occurred. As seemingly everyone glared at me, I sensed that I had caused a serious crisis of identity, that I was an emergency causing the customers to go into crisis mode. They were faced with a person who did not live by the rules established by white supremacy, a person who did not embrace the fallacy of hetero-orthodoxy. For some this became a sort of ontological negotiation, a boundary of sorts brought on by a need for the conjured reality to be that ultimate reality and

31. Homi Bhaba, *The Location of Culture*, 59.
32. Ibid.
33. Ibid.

therefore to secure them in the conjured reality approved by white supremacy.

My point is that when those considered to be the other, the unwanted, or the obscene step out of the shadows, breaking those arbitrary boundaries, into the light of divine healing, they challenge and eventually overcome the common narrative established by the oppressor, forever changing the destiny of the oppressor and themselves. I am clear that my presence in that space, which became a crisis of boundaries, also made those boundaries possibilities of what Homi Bhaba calls "hybridity." The fates of conflicting visions of humanity were in the balance as they touched at the moment at the fast food joint. "The boundary becomes a "margin of hybridity, where cultural differences 'contingently' and conflictingly touch." This margin "resists polarized political consciousness."[34] Thus, delinking American destiny from white supremacy and its power become a matter of ever increasing hybridity. This becomes the power and the implication of "coming out" that it changes the destiny of all concerned, even of God. I am presented here with an eschatological moment. It is a moment open to the provocative act of hope, that peculiar longing, even yearning for a radically different vision of humanity. Hope is that component of transformative engagement that empowers those of critical difference, even the obscene to struggle and fight for their liberation. The struggle and the fight are intimate and passionate, images of the Cross, fueled by the pain of subjection and grounded in the joy of the present-future liberation. It is what Martin Luther King, Jr. would term cruciformed living. That which once was considered obscene and a scene of subjection are now the destiny. *The formerly obscene are now the locus of legitimacy.*

This new locus of legitimacy denotes implications towards a different supporting framework of knowledge grounded in eschatological hospitality as the supporting structure of a morality that becomes the locus of this new legitimacy. This is in contrast to the previous framework of knowledge that undergirded the

---

34. Nausner. *Homeland as Borderland, Territories of Christian Subjectivity* in Postcolonial Theologies Divinity and Empire, 2004.

engagement of the "other" in the context of life and knowledge as a closed sphere of existence, a framework that embodied an ideology of critical sameness within the rubric of totalitarianism. For a moment let us look at the supporting framework of knowledge that bestows legitimacy on the current structure. It is important, even critical, to engage the framework of knowledge that supports the structures that undergird notions of legitimacy and particular ethical considerations.

Chapter 4

Reflections on Knowledge and Morality

Identity emerges out of the U.S. colonial regime as an accepted ground of discourse. It necessarily becomes a bulwark of capitalism and the political framework. It empowers the rhetoric, the dialogue and the relationship between the human and systems. Out of this predicament come definitions and images of a people who move not in their own agency or authenticity but in that which has been bestowed upon them by the colonial complex and its interlocking oppressions.

> Can identity be viewed other than a by-product of manhandling of life, one that, in fact, refers no more to a consistent pattern of sameness than to an inconsequential process of otherness?
>
> —Trinh T. Minh-ha, Filmmaker

As a consequence of who I am I often reflect on knowledge, morality and ethics. I find that because of who I am I must, at times, be mega-ethical as I live among people who I experience as being unconscious of states of being beyond the existence supported and codified by notions of white supremacy and salvation. I do ponder this framework that supports the hatred, stares and disbelief I experience each day. Pondering this unfortunate state I find some relief in Emmanuel Levinas, a gift from Professor Gabriella Lettini of Star King School for the Ministry. Emanuel Levinas was a professor at Stanford University. He was an ethicist and philosopher born in Kaunas, Lithuania in 1906.

Levinas, a precursor of James Baldwin and Cornel West, engages the other as an authentic, even a sacred presence. In his book, *Totality and Infinity*, he intimates that morality is a contextualized structure within the knowable and not the unknowable or "the other."[1] Levinas' intimation compels me to ask, "How shall morality, in the absence of the knowable, apply to the other?" Knowledge, as a supporting framework of the tribe, community and state, experienced as totality, codifies and negotiates the desires of that tribe, community or state. I am referring here to a knowledge framework of categories grounded in white supremacy that become a means of exploitation toward notions of capitalism. Knowledge embraced as essential to living under white supremacy is the very tool that maintains the oppression of the other.

This framework of knowledge, and I include biblical interpretations in this framework, is used to support the construction of a desire for the ethical and the moral within the context of white supremacy. In this context those considered deviant, i.e., unable to assimilate into whiteness, as a content of the regime, become the regimes production of transgressive performance apt for exploitation, necessarily bearing the burden of white supremacist notions of desire and as such a certain irrelevance of ethical and moral considerations. Gated communities, corporate structures, various media, education, the prison industrial complex, i.e. the dominant structures, the history constructed and the linguistics of American society tend to reflect the desires of the regime.

1. Levinas. Totality and Infinity.

Normative white supremacist desires, codified in local and national policy, i.e. immigration, education, techniques of living and a technique of existence[2], develop out of this framework of knowledge and are to be understood as the relevant and the qualified knowledge base. Knowledge which supports or advocates for the other becomes disqualified. I suggest here that "progress" and "advancement" interpreted as public policies are historically signifiers of the regime. "The disqualified knowledge, i.e. antiquated and obsolete, becomes signifiers for bygone systems of former civilizations and an incompetent, albeit ravished third world. In his book "*Society must be Defended*," Michel Foucault, noted professor and lecturer at the Collège de France from 1971 until his death in 1984 writes about subjugated knowledges. He writes, subjugated knowledges are those knowledges that have been discarded and unqualified."[3]

For Foucault these knowledges are a whole series of disqualified nonconceptual knowledges, as insufficiently elaborated knowledges; naïve knowledges, hierarchically inferior knowledges that are below that required level of erudition or scientificity.[4] Foucault's analysis of subjugated knowledge(s) further clarifies for me the relevance of knowledge(s) which undergird functional coherences or formal systematizations.

"They are blocks of historical knowledges that were present in the functional and systematic ensembles, but which were masked, and the critique was able to reveal their existence by using obviously enough the tools of scholarship."[5] Reflecting on Foucault's analysis I suggest that the treatment of knowledge must begin by looking at the desire of the "I" to dominate space, time and identity. The "I" within knowledge, rooted in American individualism, touted by Mitt Romney, the 2012 Republican Presidential candidate's statement in reference to the beginning of a business as an

2. Michele Foucault. Ethics, Subjectivity and Truth, ed. Paul Rabinow, 89.

3. Foucault. Society Must Be Defended. Lectures at the Collège De France 1975–1976, 7.

4. Ibid.

5. Ibid.

individual accomplishment versus the integration of a community of desires, becomes the pinnacle of white supremacy and patriarchy as the white settler entering foreign lands occupies a world of the unfamiliar, the unknown.[6] The "I" then, being a representation of white discourse, understands itself then as the sole figure and arbiter of authentic realities.

The "I" of white supremacy, white privilege, becomes a divine, even sacred, encounter as the story of Moses and the burning bush come to mind. In this text God says, I am that I am. (Exodus 3:14) There is then an attendant dynamic of the "I" emerging from white supremacy that is evidenced in the moral consideration imposed by the narcissistic familiar, as the familiar defines the center, the moral and the righteous.

Levinas writes, "Morality will oppose politics in history and will have gone beyond the functions of prudence or the canons of the beautiful to proclaim itself as unconditional and universal when the eschatology of messianic peace will have come to superimpose itself on the ontology war."[7] Levinas' treatment of morality as a contextualized reality within totality, under the stern arms of politics and war becomes a discourse on the familiar, the intimate, notions of sameness and their limitations, raising notions of Bonhoeffer's treatment of the ultimate and the penultimate.[8]

These limitations imposed on morality necessarily reflect the penultimate, the next to last, and not the ultimate, considered here as eschatological, the eschatological being the other or for that matter irrelevant to local considerations of communal relationships. These limitations, perceived here as final are considered as arbitrary and evidenced as a discourse on the familiar, reveal politics and war, whether cultural or societal, as structures of morality based on the intimately familiar embodied in the community. I write here of U.S. foreign policy as pertains to people in Southwest Asia, politically known as the Middle East, situated as

---

6. www.baltimoresun.com Ryan, Romney embrace a hyper-individualistic view of America's past and future accessed May 21, 2013.

7. Levinas. Totality and Infinity, 21.

8. Bonhoeffer. Dietrich Bonhoeffer Works Volume 6, Ethics, 137.

an opportunity for Jesus and his disciples to ride in on chariots of steel for the salvation of the lost.

I ask my fellows, "Can morality apply to that which is unfamiliar, to the stranger or to that which is not understood?" "Does morality stop at the front door of a sequestered imagination, denying hospitality to the enslaved, the child, the immigrant, the Muslim, and the impoverished or to a body queerly defined?" I take this perspective as an African-American shaped by the white desire for slavery, segregation, the plantation, a civil war and certain legislation, reflective of abolitionist concerns, that affirmed an historical quest to be considered human and as such a credible and ethical identity, a free "moral" agent.

I write this as a one who grew up in South Central Los Angeles in the 1960's, 1970's and 1980's, in the aftermath of the Watts Rebellion, where rampant discrimination and the resulting unemployment in the African American Community was between 20% and 30%. As I write and rewrite this paper I am reminded that the underlying conditions that spawned the Watts Rebellion are still yet present, although modified as the regime seeks to sooth the oppressed soul as a strategic move towards social and political desire. I remember years later reading about the Rodney King incident and the ensuing riots that followed and the O.J. Simpson case that became media sensations as a sailor at sea feeling the emotions of a native son. In these contexts, morality seems at times useless in a struggle against a system that fails to consider black and brown people as human beings of value. I must consider the scope of Levinas' thought in light of the shifting sands of a desert full of otherness. The poem below was written by Martin Niemöeller, a noted minister and an outspoken foe of Adolf Hitler. It speaks to the shifting sands, the embodiment of the other.

> First they came for the Socialists, and I did not speak out—
> Because I was not a Socialist.
> Then they came for the Trade Unionists, and I did not speak out—
> Because I was not a Trade Unionist.

Then they came for the Jews, and I did not speak out—Because I was not a Jew.

Then they came for me — and there was no one left to speak for me.[9]

Coming off of Niemöeller's poem the challenge presented by the presence of the other towards family, tribe and community is the communication of the beyond, of God's presence. The other presents a discourse on the need to be, it is an appeal to the eschaton, of life as a reality of God. From time to time I am confronted with the question "Why is transformation important to me, particularly in terms of race and gender?" It comes from well-meaning people who view my idea of transformation as somehow selfish, all about me since the systems and processes don't work well for me. This poem is a reminder that if I fail to stand up and do the work I do the very people who imply that I am selfish would be in danger. They would be next.

THE OTHER AND THE ESCHATON (AS REALIZED IN CHRIST) TOWARDS EMBODIMENT AND TRANSCENDENCE AND ADDRESSING THE PRODUCTION OF AN IDEOLOGY OF HATRED

A discussion of the other, their alterity, and the eschaton (as realized in Christ, the revelation of God) becomes a significant course of liberative thought as we set sail towards the shores of embodiment and transcendence. I seek to be clear and concise, as transcendence, used here as an ontological approach to morality, rather strategic, becomes a move to address occidental structures of totalitarianism and their production of an ideology of hatred.

Embodiment and transcendence regarding alterity of the other is a movement to express a certain frustration with a U.S. culture and society that seemingly embrace Aristotelian notions

---

9. The Annoying Difference: The Emergence of Danish Neonationalism, Neoracism and Populism in a Post 1989 world, ed. by Peter Hervik

of sameness and reductionism[10] as sacred constructs of divine import, experiencing the other and their corresponding difference as less than and worthy of the wrath of God. Responding to the aforementioned assertion, I enter into this discussion from a perspective of the complex, the irreducible and the complications of the human condition. The violent death of countless people who don't identify as white, male and privileged, who don't reflect the *"appropriate"* image of the narcissistic familiar, having little to no value to the regime of white supremacy, except as a means toward amassing wealth[11], consequently experience police brutality and/ or negligence, marginalization, discrimination, murder and poverty at the hands of those who would express an ideology of hatred toward the other and the alterity embodied.

Even as I write this paper I read of the tragic death of an openly gay mayoral candidate in Clarksdale, MS who was found in a Mississippi River levee unclothed[12], the death of a young African American transgender woman in Cleveland, OH, who was chained to a concrete block[13] and the escalating rates of poverty, particularly as a function of public policy[14] are just the latest examples of the implications of an ideology of hatred. This ideology of hatred, which I suggest is based on notions of righteous anger in pursuit of messianic intent, fuels a lack of apprehension and is paraded as sacred and righteous by certain elements within U.S. culture and society.

This ideology of hatred, having amassed significant support, appears as godly yet is a ruthless machine constructed for the decimation of those who would be the other and their critical difference. An overcrowded prison industrial complex, hate crimes,

10. Wardy. The Chain of Change: a Study of Aristotle's Physics VII, 334–337.

11. www.rollingstone.com. The Story of Mitt Romney and Bain Capital accessed May 21, 2013.

12. www.thegrio.com.   81-days-of-silence-why-were-speaking-up-for-marco-mcmillian accessed May 21, 2013.

13 www.eclevelander.com *accessed May 11, 2013.*

14. www.theatlantic.com accessed May 1, 2013.

and immigration are all issues which emerge out of a totalitarian regime of white supremacy and its hatred of the other. This unfortunate situation compels a longing for hope, a longing for acceptance and genuine love that goes beyond the sensibilities of sameness established as normative notions of existence. Levinas, in Totality and Infinity, argues for a radical departure from the supremacy of sameness, writing, the alterity, the radical heterogeneity of the other, is possible only if the other is other with respect to a term whose essence is to remain at the point of departure to serve as entry into the relation to be the same not relatively but absolutely.[15] For Levinas then, the agency of the other is not contingent on the desires of or for sameness, treated here by Levinas as a form of idolatry, but is external of the stream of normative modalities of identity. From this perspective the other and their alterity is an action of the eschaton and must be treated as other, absolutely, with respect to eschatological import. To be sure what lies at the ground of Levinas' advocacy for alterity rests in a certain epistemological intent that reflects the other as the proclamation of the transcendent, of the divine. Yet in this, the "other" who already "is" through categorization is made invisible.

Mayra Rivera, in *The Touch of Transcendence A Post-Colonial Theology of God*, writes"What then can be said of the other? The other in whom we are to find the gleam of transcendence is a human person in his [her] radical singularity as other."[16] She further writes, "the other does not derive from the self or from our own categories of analysis but is prior to every initiative, to all imperialism of the same."[17] Rivera's words posit notions of lands and peoples who existed prior to the arrival of the colonizer, yet, in the consciousness of the regime of colonial discovery, were not present in space and time and therefore were nonexistent. Existence in the mind of the regime emerges as the other is catalogued and categorized, consequently sequestering the other in a time and space,

15. Levinas. Totality and Infinity.

16. Rivera. The Touch of Transcendence: A Postcolonial Theology of God, 61.

17 Ibid., 61.

grounded in the established knowledge base of the regime.[18] The other is not perceived as what and who they are but as the regime desires in support of a conjured reality. They become a boundary marker for the regime, ensuring its credibility. This becomes a tenuous strategy with implications towards segregation, i.e., the ghettos and barrios constructed by the regime of white supremacy.

Without the other as a boundary marker the credibility of the regime is put into question as the other and their alterity represent transcendence, here defined as a structure for eschatological initiatives. This becomes a crisis of legitimacy for the regime. The radical singularity of the other becomes a point of contention. As such, the regime must develop different strategies to maintain their boundaries and as such its legitimacy as demonstrated by the New Jim Crow evidenced in Michelle Alexander's Book, The *New Jim Crow, Mass Incarceration in the Age of Colorblindness*.[19]

Based on the regime's historical need for the other I suggest here that an ideology of hatred is part of an overall strategy to maintain those boundaries. The other then is the supreme provocateur, I write here, thinking of Angela Davis, James Cone, Tim Wise, James Baldwin, Elle Wiesel, and the Black Panthers, giving the clarion call to shake the foundations,[20] necessarily recognizing the power of deviancy as a divine attribute towards resistance, releasing compelling notions of the Christ narrative. Levinas writes in *Ethics as First Philosophy*, one has to respond to one's right to be, not by referring to some abstract and anonymous law or judicial entity but because of one's fear for the other, and this is Jesus as the radical. The words of Levinas become a ground of protest as the other presents the regime with a counter discourse on power, legitimacy and the body as sacred space. The words of Levinas intimate self-awareness and a particular obligation by the

18. McClintock. Imperial Leather: Race, Gender, and Sexuality in the Colonial Context.

19. Alexander. The New Jim Crow, Mass Incarceration in the Age of Colorblindness.

20. Gorsline. Shaking the Foundations. White Supremacy in the Theological Academy in The Levinas Reader. Ethics as First Philosophy, 82.

other to their alterity, even to Rivera's gleam of transcendence. These thoughts pose important considerations with regard to the embodiment of the sacred, whether bodily or systemically, and to political, cultural and social movements. Transcendence and alterity, the radical singularity, are obligations of the "other"; in this I think Angela Davis and James Cone would insist. The other must be, absolute, and this beyond reproach.

Chapter 5

Locating the Divine Transgender Feminine and the Sacred Black Masculine within a Queer Post-Colonial Architecture

There was always something wrong with how I was invented and meant to fit in the world. Whether this was because I constantly misread my part or because of some deep flaw in my being I could not tell for most of my early life. Sometimes I was intransigent, and proud of it. At other times I seemed to myself nearly devoid of any character at all—timid, uncertain, without will. Yet the overriding sensation I had was of always being out of place.[1]

—EDWARD SAID

At one point in Wole Soyinka's novel *The Interpreters,* the African-American homosexual Joe Golder, who incidentally also happens to be an historian on Africa, attempts to discuss indigenous homosexuality with Nigerian journalist Sagoe: "Do you think I know nothing of your Emirs and their little boys? You forget history is my subject. And what about the exclusive coteries

1. Said. *Out of Place: A Memoir*, 3.

66

in Lagos? Sagoe gesture(s) in defeat. "You seem better informed than I am. But if you don't mind let me persist in my delusion.

—SOYINKA, 199

The construction of the colonial subject in discourse, and the exercise of colonial power through discourse, demands an articulation of forms of difference—racial and sexual. Such an articulation becomes crucial if it is held that the body is always simultaneously (if conflictually) inscribed in both the economy of pleasure and desire and the economy of discourse, domination and power.[2]

—HOMI BHABA

We gender-variant are, like all human beings, complex and unique. We are straight, gay, and bisexual, cross-dressers, pre-operative and non-operative and intersexuals of many types, drag queens and kings; female and male illusionists; androgynous persons and other gender outlaws of various kinds. Society considers us to be nonconformists, cultural rebels who somehow manage to transcend, transgress, alter, blur, or confuse the usual categories of gender.

To the exasperation of gender traditionalists, we remain human beings who are created in the image of God, which make us intrinsically valuable and eternally loved by our creator. We are indeed as the psalmist wrote, "fearfully and wonderfully made." (Ps. 239:14)[3]

Queer Post-Colonial Architecture presents a frame or apparatus to *reclaim* the images, longings and visions of an incarnated humanity from the vestiges of white supremacy and the various modes of colonization. Arising from a hermeneutic of the oppressed, it engages a different knowledge complex. As such it seeks to locate the Divine Transgender Feminine and the Sacred Black Masculine as a fluid, ambiguous, non-exploitive spectrum

2. Bhabha. *The Locations of Culture*, 96.
3. Mollenkott and Sheridan. *Transgender Journeys*, 89.

of the infinite. Queer Post-Colonial Architecture is invitational in its identity, complex and infinite in its capacity to hold the sacred holiness embodied in the divine incarnation.

My thoughts on a Queer Post-Colonial Architecture are inspired by Virginia RameyMollenkott and Vanessa Sheridan's book entitled *"Transgender Journeys"* and the chapter entitled *"Reclaiming Our Territory, Mapping Our Pathway."*[4] As the title suggests, the work is about reclaiming and remapping our territory. It is about "resignifying gender"[5] from modes and notions of displacement, reconstruction, and delusion referenced in Said, Bhaba and, Gaurav Desai –– within an architecture of capitalization and profit to an inclusive fluid architecture reflective of an imagination motivated by love and the art of queer hospitality. It is a matter of spirit and soul, the mystical transformation of God and humanity and their intent.

Sitting on a San Francisco BART train in the midst of hundreds of people of various identities, i.e. genders, sexualities, nationalities and ethnicities, I am mindful of the delicate balance of identity and the significant weight experienced by some people, considered in this work as social constructions, to maintain the fallacy of some type of gender stabilization for the sake of a cohesive society codified by some as a sacred biblical imperative.

As a matter of cultural and historical concern, I ask, "How long can this weight be maintained before it becomes unbearable?" Encountering this question, I have become mindful of a shifting and merging and moving of civilizations, like tectonic plates, creating new and different terrains of ontological presence. Cracks, fissures and fault lines become queer fluid spaces of a steadfast hope as the other presents the cusp of an unfolding, fluid narrative of Mother Earth. The other then, through their critical difference possesses agency to bring awareness to the unconscious, and this even to the soul of the human condition.

As such, I suggest here that gender fluidity, as a representation of the other, is aligned with Mother Earth, her fluidity, and her

4. Mollenkott and Sheridan. Transgender Journeys, 89.

5. Pui-lan. *Postcolonial Imagination & Feminist Theology*, 128.

fluid expressions and as such is in a state of solidarity and oneness. Not being at odds or in competition with Mother Earth, the one who is gender fluid can be an agent of holistic presence, an appeal of Mother Earth. This is in contrast to living as an appeal of economic systems constructed to be at odds and exploitive of the earth imagined in binary economic thoughts and concepts, echoes of an oppressive interpretation of Genesis 1:27–31 by certain sects of Christianity.

As a process, Queer Post-Colonial Architecture is a turning to a discourse on sustainability and away from exploitation based systems, of which gender and sexuality are an integral part, with their interlocking oppressions to an environment that is earth-centric and liberative. This thought arises from the writings of Joanna Macy and her book *"Coming Back to Practices to Reconnect Our Lives, Our World."*[6]

> *I call heaven and earth to record this day to your account, that I have set before your life and death, blessing and curs-ing, there choose life, that both you and your seed shall live. (Deut.3:19)*[7]

From a queer postcolonial liberation perspective Macy's book is an active witness of what she terms a "Great Turning." It is considered a choice for life. For Macy, "To choose life means to build a life-sustaining society.[8] Simply put, it is a choice for a sustainable world versus an unsustainable world, a turning away from the industrial growth society to one that is in sync with the earth, a returning to the roots of human existence. It is recognition that the soul has needs beyond the consumerist-oriented notions of satisfaction.

Reflecting on Macy's *Great Turning*, I am mindful of Simone Weil's book entitled *"Needs of the Soul."*[9] Up out of the mire the

6. Macy and Brown. *Coming Back to Life, Practices to Reconnect Our Lives, Our World.*

7. Ibid., 15.

8. Ibid., 57.

9. Weil, The Need for Roots, 3—39.

question emerges, "What does the soul need in the midst of a great turning? I think this question critical as a new paradigm comes to maturity. Needs of the soul present an unconditional reality bringing forth obligations which emerge with particular ethical dimensions. With Weil's *Needs of the Soul* in mind, the intent of the Great Turning focuses on a calling to a different ontological cognizance that embraces the human and Mother Earth as a miracle, a creation emerging from the infinite.

What I mean is that there is a new consciousness on the horizon which reconnects the people with Mother Earth. Calling people to experience themselves and Mother Earth as a miracle not out of some conjured self-centered delusional capitalist profit construct but as the present intimacy of the infinite, and this beyond notions of sectarian sacredness. There is an emerging voice grounded in a different cognizance representative of a queer postcolonial spiritual and intellectual quest, this quest engendering a different imagination of ontological presence. The experience then of the divine black transgender feminine and the sacred black masculine, interpreted here as a non-conformist entity, become an intimate expression of that Great Turning as it deconstructs the binary gender regime and, as a consequence, a particular belief system that abuses Mother Earth and her offspring. The Great Turning presents a question of *sustainability*. "Is our present state of human affairs sustainable?"

The whole of this project is grounded in this one important quest, to find and do what is sustainable. This question is posed seemingly on a daily basis as each day there are reports of more and more people coming out of the binary regime, challenging traditional gender religious and political discourse.

Transitions don't occur because of some senseless selfish notion of privilege but for survival, even of sustainability. This quest becomes the passion, even the Christ of life, that life is defined as a discourse on sustainability. There is a realization that sustainability should negotiate practical concerns as it is the practical and, in some sense, the logical that must be revered. Yet I suggest that notions of the practical must be recalibrated so as to be in concert with life-affirming and life-giving structures, and in this sense sustainable.

This is a challenging call for communities whose notions of sustainability are narrowly defined as structures of privilege and power. Sustainability is communal; it is about the whole of humanity and not one particular privileged population of people. Sustainability must be the new ground of politics, religion and the corporate community. Beloved, each day is a call for sustainability as society copes with a broken education system, rising suicide rates, drug abuse, ethical concerns and challenges, and issues of life and death. All of these discussions revolve around the issues and concerns of sustainability. Discussions of gender, sexuality and marriage equality are mere distractions from a very real discussion of sustainability.

Sustainability is the foundational discourse of Queer Postcolonial architecture and as such it becomes a discourse in authenticity. Authenticity and its various dynamics including healing ultimately culminate in notions of sustainability.

Chapter 6

Sustainability and the Beloved Community, a Sacred Discourse

All that Jazz

"The fullness of divine import is experienced as the "I" embraces
that which sustains *its* sacred holy presence."

—Anonymous

Through my years in Christendom, communion has become a
discourse on sustainability. A mystical symbol of Jesus' love, it
is a most intimate encounter which sustains me as I move through
the joys, hopes, sorrows and challenges of the day. Communion
is transcendent, unveiling God's longing for the oppressed and
the oppressor. It holds the infinite and the finite, it is everlasting
and this without sway. Living a life of communion, I address those
deeper truths, issues, concerns and questions of sustainability.
Questions such as, "How do I sustain myself, my community and
those relationships significant to me on this journey? How do I live
an authentic life yet somehow balance that authenticity with the
grace and mercy for others and myself without finding myself in a
space of the inauthentic?"

These questions emerge as a primary consequence of my experience of identity. This has been an intensely personal unfolding, and I might add, a public witness of sacred import as relationships in community, culture, society and the political reveal themselves and their limits to me, each becoming a discourse on the challenges of inclusivity, sustainability, and strategies to life, agency and power. Identity, i.e. gender, sexuality, race, economics, immigration and the environment then must be viewed as concerns and challenges of human sustainability and in this sense a call to return to earth embodiment.

These words present a call for a different hope, one not shaped by the present political theology and its advocacy of a profit-based economics sustained by a particular pathology of violence upon non-hetero-normative identities and a coddling of the simple minded but a hope which embodies a queer hospitality grounded in infinity with a goal of sustainability. In this I am mindful of Hannah Arendt and her treatment of political legitimacy and its implications toward revolutionary intent. Based on her words sustainability becomes a conversation on civil disobedience.

This may sound odd but, in a world of the heteronormative, the materialistic and the associated idolatry, an authenticity which does not reflect this reality can be detrimental to life, liberty and just plain survival. In this light a conversation on sustainability continues the courageous work of justice as a sacred discourse within the Civil Rights Movement. Issues of identity, i.e. race, poverty, education, gender and sexuality are all sacred historical conversations of justice; in this I suggest sustainability. Pushing this conversation further, I suggest here that sustainability becomes a conversation of the "I" and its holiness. It becomes a sacred challenge to established systems of community which shape desires of the religious, economy and the political.

Now emerging from a cultural and historical perspective, I long for the abstract, even the complex, not to be the enemy of the accessible since it is the abstract and the complex which more intimately embraces the authenticity, even the truth of the human condition, and this becomes my argument; my push for sustainability. Identity is intimately engaged in the project of sustainability and as such becomes a discourse on eschatology and in this sense it is that primary transformational presence moving culture and society towards new horizons of hope.

Horizons of hope rest in an uncommon faith which emerges out of our intimate relationship with the divine. It is a faith that yields a courage grounded in the garden of Gethsemane and expressed on the Cross. It is compelling and unrelenting, moving the sojourner through space and time, through struggle and joy to affect the divine cosmic human interaction. Sustainability, then, emerging as an activity of this uncommon faith, becomes an orientation to the limitless love of God. Sustainability must be a provocative act, an expression of heart and soul and the meaning of a beloved community.

The beloved community, experienced as a dynamic gathering of hearts, is intimately engaged in a discourse on sustainability as thoughts of critical difference; togetherness and radical inclusivity become the primary means for maintaining the beloved community. Sustainability of relationships becomes a ground of relational improvisation as those who embrace the ideals of a beloved community seek to make it real in space and time. Building and maintaining relationships in community must be a sacred act of love, taking on the character and the image of the Christ reality.

The Christ reality is personal and communal; it is authentic, embracing the individual's authentic space of being within the communal. It is a most intimate affair, a root of empowerment and a critical element within a discourse on sustainability. I experience my church as a culture of sustainability. It is dynamic, post-colonial, multicultural and post-structuralist; exhibiting the mosaic of a Holy God. A sacred space of authenticity and radical inclusivity, it is a community of faith where the person of faith practices various forms of ontological mediation. Professor Michael Eric Dyson, one of the most talented intellectuals and a rhetorical acrobat, writes in his essay *Baptizing Theory, Representing the Truth* the following regarding ontological mediation, "Ontological negotiation stresses how black narratives help construct relations between beings: horizontal relations between human beings and vertical relations between human beings. Black religious discourse helps define, and mediate the moral status of human existence."[1]

Taken further I suggest that ontological negotiation might apply to all people who value their particular narrative. This becomes a space where a whole lot of prayer, grace and mercy are necessary for the nourishment of the beloved community. Bring your truth, even your authenticity, and let us talk and fellowship in togetherness. At times this may require some improvisation[2] as those who seek to build the beloved community engage in creating a space of harmony even with a dissonance that harmonizes with the call of God. As each person offers their authentic selves the beloved community appears first as the love of Christ and secondly as a protest against the supremacy of the normative established by and for the sanctity of culture and society. More than anything else the beloved community and sustainability is a life affirming narrative of God.

Theologically, the beloved community is provocative and hopeful, an expressed joy of divine import. Emerging out of Rev. Dr. Martin Luther King, the beloved community presents a community of beatitudinal realities where those identified in Matthew 5:1–12 long for various forms of spiritual, emotional and mental sustainability. Reflecting for a moment on a culture and society that lives in the reflection of the proverbial mirror, the beloved community seeks to reflect the God of all that is. In this sense the credibility of the beloved community rests in God and the Cross of Jesus, and this is also its portion. This is in contrast to culture and society whose credibility rests in the limitations found in its own reflection. The beloved community, a practical and revolutionary act of human and divine sustainability, is a sacred space of the infinite and in this sense a most intimate construct of God consciousness.

1. Dyson. *Baptizing Theory, representing the Truth in Open Mike Reflections on Philosophy, sex, race, culture and Religion*, 43.

2. Dyson. *The Great Next in Open Mike Reflections on Philosophy, sex, race, culture and Religion*, 179–206.

Chapter 7

Conclusion

S itting here at the local Starbucks, the questions which long to be answered are, "What shall be said at the conclusion of the whole matter? What have I, as the writer, been seeking to communicate in this book?" In response to this question I find that I am compelled to search my thoughts to attempt to provide some type of response to the heart and soul of the reader, a challenging task indeed. Yet, to not at least give it the good old college try denies the importance I feel for the reader. So here we go.

This book is an outpouring of study, reflection, dynamic and at times intense relationships with God and community. It is a product of life experience and a whole lot of faith and prayer. It emerges from experiences of the intersections, i.e. identity; gender, race, sexuality, economy, and a relationship with the divine that is seldom understood yet so very present in the life of the writer and their imagination. This book is somewhat of a call, if you will, regarding the ongoing struggle for liberation, justice and sustainability. I need you, the reader, to be conscious, not just of the oppressions encountered at the surface level but at a deep embodied level so that change would not just be philosophical or academic but physical and practical.

The work of justice means very little without a narrative of physicality. That said, this book is grounded in theology, yet engaged in cultural and historical discourses which have revolutionary and political intent as a divine calling. At a personal level I do experience reading and as such critical thinking as experiences of a divine calling simply because the two are some of the actions that can lead to real and genuine liberation and, in this sense, transformation. It is hoped that each person reading this book would intentionally and seriously engage the text and as such receive their truth, authenticity and embrace once again their divinity. Only then can there be real and undeniable change. In this sense the reader becomes the ground, even the origin of a new order, even a new movement for change and transformation. Reading can be a revolutionary act if employed in the service of liberation.

There were several goals in mind for this book, which made it worth writing. The first goal was to create a space for *Coming Out*. This coming out, not being just about gender and sexuality but a coming out of a mindset, a pathology that employs various oppressions which intersect necessarily causing physical, emotional, mental and spiritual contexts that are actually unsustainable. The second goal was to call the reader to embrace memory as a profound teacher of knowledge and wisdom towards real and undeniable liberation. A third goal of this book was to liberate the body and the terms of the body from the perspective of a profit-oriented racial hetero-patriarchy to a post-colonial queer architecture of fluidity.

To delink from notions of white supremacy, white privilege. and supporting knowledges,to develop and create a new space of legitimacy, where those formerly identified as the "other" become the ground of that new space of legitimacy. The fourth and probably the most important goal of this book was to create a mental space which would compel the reader to utilize their liberation to reconnect with the earth as a matter of earth and human sustainability. In this sense it is ultimately a book immersed in a narrative of healing.

Reflecting for a moment on those notions of practicality I must caution the reader that liberation is rarely ever received as practical. Simply put, it goes against a particular mindset that advocates for stability, sameness and "don't rock the boat." So ideas and concepts of liberation, although hardly any context would exist without the compelling narrative of liberation, becomes a call to go beyond the reader's comfort zone. Practicality, in the context of a struggle and fight for liberation has a very real potential to become another form of enslavement. When in the process of building a movement, critical thinking is the hope and nourishment of the liberated soul. The practical then, if not critically engaged, can be a means of deception and as such must be viewed with suspicion.

This book provides an opportunity to see life from a very different angle, one that I hope is life affirming and sustainable for the reader. And this is the aim, even the goal, that the reader would receive themselves and their divinity as the truth, and with this an empowerment of their liberation. Beloved, I think this to be the ground of all liberative discourse, that through our embrace as the divine we are compelled to fight and struggle for liberation. A person who has encountered and embraced their liberation, engaging in a critical faith becomes a great and unyielding fear for the oppressor.

Bibliography

Abraham, Laurie. She's All That. Interview with WNBA player Brittney Griner in November 2013 issue of Elle.

Alexander, Michelle. The New Jim Crow, Mass Incarceration in the Age of Colorblindness. New York, NY: The New Press, 2010.

Althaus-Reid, Marcella. Indecent Theology Theological Perversions in Sex, Gender and Politics. New York, NY: Routledge

Baldwin, James. On being White and Other Lies: The White World and Whiter World. New York, NY: Orbis, 1987.

Bhaba, Homi. The Locations of Culture New York, NY: Routledge, 1994.

Bonhoeffer, Dietrich. Dietrich Bonhoeffer Works Volume 6, Ethics. Minneapolis, Augsburg-Fortress, 2005.

Brown, Karen McCarthy. Mama Lola, A Voduo Priestess in Brooklyn. Berkeley, CA: University of California Press, 1991.

Butler, Judith. Bodies that Matter, On the Discursive Limits of Sex. New York, NY: Routledge, 1993.

Cone, James. The Cross and the Lynching Tree. Maryknoll, NY: Orbis, 2011.

Copeland, M Shawn. Enfleshing Freedom, Body, Race and Being. Minneapolis, MN: Fortress Press, 2010.

Desmond, Jenée. Please Stop Assuming all Blacks are Christian, Race Manners: The Good News About Being an Atheist Who's Annoyed by this Stereotype is that You're Not Alone. The Root accessed October 11, 2013.

Fluker, Walter E. and Catherine Tumber, eds. A Strange Freedom: The Best of Howard Thurman on Religious Experience and Public Life. Boston, MA: Beacon, 1998.

Foucault, Michel. Society Must be Defended. Lectures at the College De France 1975–1976. New York, NY: Picador, 1997.

Foucault, Michel. Ethics, Subjectivity and Truth. Edited by Paul Rabinow. New York, NY: The New, 1994.

Gorsline, Robin H. Shaking the White Foundations, White Supremacy in the Theological Academy in Disrupting White Supremacy from Within: White People on What We Need to Do. Edited by Jennifer Harvey, Karin A. Case, and Robin Hawley Gorsline. Pilgrim, 2004.

Bibliography

Hooks, Bell. *Outlaw Culture: Resisting Representations*. New York, NY: Routledge, 1994.

Levinas, Emmanuel. *Totality and Infinity*. Boston, MA: Martinus Nijhoff, 1979.

———. *Ethics as First Philosophy in the Levinas Reader*. Edited by Sean Hand. Cambridge, MA: Blackwell, 1989.

Macy, Joanna and Molly Brown. *Coming Back to Life, Practices to Reconnect Our Lives, Our World*. Gabriola, BC: New Society, 1998.

McClintock, Anne. *Imperial Leather: Race, Gender, and Sexuality in the Colonial Context*. New York, NY: Routledge, 1995.

Mollenkott, Virginia Ramey and Vanessa Sheridan. *Transgender Journeys*, Cleveland, OH: Pilgrim, 2003.

Niemöeller, Martin. *The Annoying Difference: The Emergence of Danish Neonationalism, Neoracism and Populism in a Post 1989 World*. Edited by Peter Hervik. New York, NY: Berghahn, 2011.

Pui-lan, Kwok. *Postcolonial Imagination & Feminist Theology*. Louisville, KY: Westminster John Knox, 2005.

Reid-Rivera, Mayra. *The Touch of Transcendence: A Postcolonial Theology of God*. Louisville, KY: Westminster John Knox, 2007.

Said, Edward. *Out of Place: A Memoir*. New York, NY: Random, 2000.

Wardy, Robert. *The Chain of Change: a Study of Aristotle's Physics VII*. Cambridge Classic Studies Pp x + 345; 2 figures. Cambridge University Press, 1990.

Wilkerson, Isabel. *The Warmth of Other Suns*. New York, NY: Random House, 2011.

www.advocate.com. Transgender Woman's Body Found Near Cleveland; News Coverage Denounced accessed May 1, 2013.

www.boomantribune.com. Racism in a straight line accessed May 6, 2013.

www.theatlantic.com. The Ghetto is Public Policy accessed May 1, 2013.

www.thegrio.com. 81-days-of-silence-why-we're-speaking-up-for-marco-mcmillian accessed May 21, 2013.

www.rollingstone.com. The Story of Mitt Romney and Bain Capital accessed May 21, 2011.

www.presidency.ucsb.edu. President Lyndon B. Johnson State of the Union of speech *of 1965* accessed May 6, 2013.

www.youtube.com. Segregation at all Costs: Bull Conner and the Civil Rights Movement accessed May 6, 2013.

Index

Index